Becoming The Blessing God Intended for My Family

Becoming The Blessing God Intended for My Family

The Christ-Centered Family

Miracle O.A. Bashorun
Deborah L. Bashorun

To order additional copies of this book, contact:
Xlibris
1-888-795-4274
www.Xlibris.com
Orders@Xlibris.com
766138

CONTENTS

About Miracle Ministry

Miracle Ministry is founded upon the Lord Jesus Christ's command to preach the gospel unto the uttermost parts of the earth (Acts 1:8). As ambassadors for Christ, we are in the ministry of reconciliation (2 Corinthians 5:18-21). The vision of the ministry is to spread the water of life to every nation until the trump of God shall sound to rapture His saints.

Some segments or activities of the Miracle Ministry include: Miracle Radio Station (where people will tune in to and receive encouragement in their situations, salvation, Holy Ghost baptism, deliverance and healing in Jesus' name); "The More Excellent Way" (anointed television programs) and Hephzibah Crusades (regular gathering of blood washed believers and unsaved precious souls to experience the power of God, possess all that was made available on the cross of Calvary by the shed blood of the lamb, and receive the touch of the Holy Spirit which would result in salvation, healing, deliverance, resurrection from the dead, etc.). Also, water baptism will be conducted regularly for those who have received Christ as Lord and

Savior in any of our programs around the world and it will be broadcasted on television for the world to see that their identity has been changed. Halleluyah!

Surely, the dead will be raised back to life (Hebrews 11:35), the lame will walk, the blind will see, the oppressed shall be delivered, sinners shall be converted, the kingdom of darkness will tremble and the name of the Lord will be praised (Psalm 113:3)!

Even so Lord, let it be. (Amen).

DEDICATION

This book is dedicated to our heavenly Father, the giver of godly wisdom and insight on training godly kids and future leaders to impact the world for God.

Acknowledgement

We acknowledge the Lord Jesus Christ and the blessed Holy Spirit for giving us the inspiration and instruction to write this book. He alone is worthy to be praised forevermore!

Also, we will like to specially acknowledge our dear brother, Dave Morgan for his dear support and impact in our life and destiny. Truly, he has been an instrument of God.

Special acknowledgement goes to our "Future Leaders" – Anointed, Hosanna, Zion and Glorious. These are the leaders of tomorrow and play an important role in our lives as our children.

We also want to acknowledge everyone who has in one way or the other contributed to the materialization of this publication. I thank all involved in the publishing; and every other contributor to this success. My God shall surely reward you.

Last but surely not the least; we specially say a big thank you to all blood washed believers who have imparted into our lives via their prayers, contributions, words of encouragement, exhortations and many other ways. Some of these saints include: Phil and LuVenia Howse; *Kemi Toki; Greg and Esther Volmar; Sharon and Jennifer Salu; Ike and *Seun Alakija; *Gbenga and Kemi Fadahunsi; April and June Walker; Hilton Harrell; Patrick and Karine Backer; Pastor Remegio Blanco; Pastor Toks Idowu; Stuart and Vickie Carver; Lisa Braxton; Mike and Tina Lockhart; Jennifer Repko-Nowlin; and much, much more! Your reward is great in heaven.

*Deceased

INTRODUCTION

Purpose of the book

This book is written to pour out a lot of what God in His Divine Excellency has deposited within us that all might be richly blessed. A lot from our personal meditations, life experiences, lessons from saints of God, and much more are included so that every reader will be able to draw from the well of life.

Upon completion of the book, the reader should have a fresh insight on the Christ-centered family which will inspire them to build (or rebuild) their family on Christ the rock, and our firm foundation.

We pray that the wisdom of God will guide you as you read through the pages of this book.

Overview

This book brings to light, years of divine revelation on marriage and family. Furthermore, personal experiences that the authors have learned from, are used to expose more on the plan of God for family. The book will dig deep into the divine role that each member of the family has to play, to create and experience 'the Christ centered family' that God intended for every marriage and family.

When God told Abraham: "And I will make of thee a great nation, and I will bless thee, ... and thou shalt be a blessing" (Genesis 12:2), the blessing and greatness started in the family. Acts 1:8 declares: "But ye shall receive power, after that the Holy Ghost is come upon you: and ye shall be witnesses unto me both in Jerusalem, and in all Judaea, and in Samaria, and unto the uttermost part of the earth" – Jerusalem, before Judea, then Samaria, then the uttermost part of the earth. The blessing of God can start small (within the family), before it expands to the whole earth! That is why it is important to pay critical attention to how to groom a godly family for the glory of God.

We have often heard that "the family that prays together, stays together". Praying together and building a family based on divine principles from God's word, is a sure path to grooming a family for exploits in God (Daniel 11:32). God said of Abraham: "For I know him, that he will command his children and his household after him, and they shall keep the way of the Lord, to do justice and judgment; that the Lord may bring upon Abraham that which he hath spoken of him" (Genesis 18:19).

We pray that you be richly blessed as you read this book.

CHAPTER 1

(BECOMING THE BLESSING GOD INTENDED FOR MY SPOUSE)

"For this cause shall a man leave his father and mother, and cleave to his wife..." Mark 10:7

The True Meaning and Purpose of Marriage

When I was growing up, little girls and boys would play "house" and pretend to be married. If you were to ask little girls in my generation about their future, most would tell you the name of their "future husbands" and how many children they wanted. In this generation, the perspective of marriage has drastically changed. I recently surveyed several classes of middle school students about their future aspirations. Sadly, most of them said they wanted nothing to do with marriage, but all of them wanted children. When I asked them why they didn't want to get married, many were disillusioned with the existence of so much divorce and feared that this fate was just inevitable. Then the tables were turned on me; a student asked: "with everybody getting divorced, why should I get married?" The question echoed in my heart like the distant cry of an explorer lost in a dark empty cave. It was a good and thought-provoking question. Why should anyone get married? What is the purpose of marriage? Is it something to check off my list? Is it to have someone fill the empty space in my bed? Is it to have someone to share the bills with? Or, is it to have someone make my food and clean up after me? The purpose of marriage is far deeper than any superficial physical need. Marriage is the only relationship that God uses to exemplify our union with Christ (Isaiah. 62:5, Matthew 9:15, Matthew 25:1-13). He is the bridegroom and we as the church are His bride. God, therefore, uses strong marriages and families to spread the message of His love in the Earth and to set the standard for others to attain. A **strong marriage** witnesses Christ's love to children who have to daily battle negative influences and the temptations to go down the wrong path. When children grow up in godly homes with godly marriages, they are built to carry on a legacy of love and unity that continuously lays a foundation for future generations to stand on. Simply put, biblical reasons for marriage are friendship and companionship; fruitfulness and multiplication; support in vision and destiny; building up another godly generation; and reflecting Christ's relationship with the church.

In the beginning of the book of Genesis, God describes the beauty of the land of Eden. From the brilliantly incandescent stars in the heavens to the lush green vegetation right at his fingertips, Adam was surrounded by all the glory of God's wonderous creation and yet, God still saw that something was missing. He said in Genesis 2:18: "It is not good (or beneficial) that the man should be alone; I will make him an help meet for him". In the Amplified Version, it says: "...I will make him a helper [one who balances him— a counterpart who is] suitable and complimentary for him". Another version (New English Translation) says: "...I will make a companion for him who corresponds to him". Correspond means to be in agreement, to be in tune with, or to be in harmony with. God, in His infinite wisdom, saw that two walking in unity was better than one. This is not to say that God has not given some the grace to live a single life unto Him as we see this example with Apostle Paul. However, God knew that there is more strength in the unity of brethren joining together. In the book of Ecclesiastes 4:9-12 says that: "Two are better than one; because they have a good reward for their labor. For if they fall, the one will lift up his fellow: but woe to him that is alone when he falleth; for he hath not another to help him up. Again, if two lie together, then they have heat: but how can one be warm alone?" Essentially, when a man and woman unite in marriage, they serve as lifelines for one another as they journey through the mountains and valleys of human existence; undoubtedly an often arduous journey to complete alone. As a wife or a husband, you become the driving force that helps propel your mate into their destiny. However, this gigantic task can only be accomplished when the both of you are anchored in the grace of God. So, the very nature of marriage is to establish you in a triune (father-spouse-you) relationship that provides support and meets the essential needs: belonging, fellowship, protection. In a marriage where God is the covering, center, and foundation, both people experience the same type of comfort and support as young children holding their mother's hand crossing a busy intersection. There is security in surrendering our everything to Him. If you notice, the triune relationship has the father (God) as the first, the spouse as the second in the chain and you as the last in the chain. In order to experience true or divine "**JOY**" in any marital relationship, **J**esus must be first, **O**thers (in this case, your spouse) must be second, and **Y**ourself last.

Furthermore, on the purpose and meaning of marriage, **to understand the significance of your spouse, you need to understand the difference between family and blood. There is a difference between family and blood. Family is not necessarily your blood and blood is not always your family. Family is more significant or deeper than blood. Joseph's brothers were his blood, but they did not treat him as family, not even as a friend. Esau and Jacob were blood, but they did not always act as family. David and Jonathan were not blood, but they acted like brothers (family). Even Joseph, the father of Jesus was Jesus' father, but had no blood connection to Jesus. Your wife is the closest family to you, but she is not your blood. However, she is your flesh and your bone (Genesis 2:21-23). As a matter of fact, she is one with you and you are one with her (Genesis 2:24)!**

"And Enoch walked with God...." Genesis 5:24

Pre-Marriage

Isn't it funny how some of the most seemingly simple things come with instructions? I even once read directions on a canned drink: "Pop the top. Sip. Enjoy!" So, it's a wonder, with a world full of instruction manuals, GPS, and directions, why wouldn't there be anything to help guide people who want to get married? Or is there? The Bible is truly our instruction manual for life and if we look closely it also gives explicit guidance for singles who are marriage-minded! As singles, we should be like Enoch who walked with God by relying on His manual (the bible) for instructions in every area of life, especially in the choice of a life partner.

The Bible commands every Christian to pray without ceasing (1 Thessalonians 5:17). Therefore, one of the greatest steps a single person can do to prepare for marriage is not getting a job, or a larger bank account, or a beautiful white gown or perfectly tailored suit. The greatest thing they can ever do is prepare spiritually by becoming a warrior on their knees. This is especially true for women, who become "keepers of the home", according to Titus 2:5. Just as gate keepers are to a house, "keepers of the home" help set the atmosphere of their home and guard what is allowed in their home. They act as watchmen observing influences surrounding their husband and children; and learn how to pray and commit their home to God. They know, as the word says, "… except the Lord keep the city, the watchman waketh but in vain" (Psalm 127:1). Therefore, to operate in such a vital role, one needs to prepare beforehand. When individuals train to become a part of the military, they go and grow through a grueling training process designed to prepare them for the battlefield. They complete exercises to help build their strength and endurance and build their resolve to fight…. no matter the enemy… no matter the obstacle….period. Without this training, a soldier would flee the battlefield very quickly during a grueling enemy assault. Learning to pray in singleness is advantageous and will arm you and prepare you to respond in a tactical manner when the weapons have been drawn and you are under attack.

You think you want "tall, dark and handsome"? What you see is not always what you get! We as a society spend a lot of time and money on our appearances. Billions upon billions of dollars are spent on cosmetics, clothing, perfumes, hair, and surgeries to cover up flaws and fit into the mold of popular opinion. In the end you have people who are aesthetically pleasing to "Your beauty should not come from outward adornment, such as elaborate hairstyles and the wearing of gold jewelry or fine clothes. Rather, it should be that of your inner self, the unfading beauty of a gentle and quiet spirit, which is of great worth in God's sight" (1 Peter 3:3-4, NIV). When we are searching for a mate, our primary concern should not be the physical appearance. Having that shallow perspective can be deceptive and detrimental to our futures. What we see is not all always what we get. God teaches us this wisdom through the experience of the prophet Samuel. Samuel, though a man who sought God and communed with Him, was still being led by his eyes when he was searching for a King. Samuel saw "tall, dark, and handsome" and automatically made his assumption that this has got to be the one! But look at what God says: "But the LORD said unto Samuel, Look not on his countenance, or on the height of his stature; because I have refused him: for *the LORD seeth* not as man seeth; for man looketh on the outward appearance, but the LORD looketh on the heart" (1 Samuel 16:7).

When a man is **lured** by a woman, he says anything to her, he makes promises to her, he does anything for her in the moment; but generally, all that he says and does is temporal and insincere. As such, the woman ends up hurt. When a man **finds** a woman, he loves her and whatever he says to her when he loves her, he tries his very best to fulfill not just momentarily, but as long as he possibly can. That is the difference between love and lure (or lust)! Therefore, it is better for a woman to be found than to lure a man with her body. When a man is lured to a woman, other women will also try to lure him, which makes the relationship fragile. Once he is lured by another woman, he moves on. However, when a man finds (and loves) a woman, other women may come to lure him, but he will have more of a desire for what he found therefore resisting the lure. Even if he falls, his desire will still be with what he found (Proverbs 24:16). Finding takes time, lusting comes easy. More so, what a person has to really search and dig for, is more valuable and precious because it is rare and special!

In the process of finding a spouse, it is important that singles should not be jumping in and out of relationships, but prayerfully find the right one at the right time. This avoids dealing with numerous heart breaks that worldly dating has to offer. It is important to wait to find God's choice when one is prepared and ready for marriage before you begin a courtship and the eventual marriage. When we follow God's guidelines for choosing a life partner, we see that finding the right partner in marriage is a simpler process than what many may experience. **Finding and marrying the right partner was intended to be a quick and easy process**. Adam's marriage was quick, Jacob's marriage was quick, etc. Therefore, it is God's plan and intention for us to have a quick process in finding and settling down in marriage. However, *it is just the human factor and sinful or deceptive nature of man, that makes it expedient to take more time to find out who the other person really is (in godly courtship) before getting married.* Just as in divorce, Jesus told the Pharisees that "...Moses <u>because of the hardness of your hearts</u> suffered you to put away your wives: <u>but from the beginning it was not so</u>" (Matthew 19:8). Also, with regards to the ease and simplicity of finding a spouse, having difficulty and going through a tedious process was not the way it was from the beginning! Adam did not have a courtship, neither did Isaac.

In finding a spouse, the woman is to present herself or make herself available, while the man is to ask or speak. Eve presented herself to Adam by God, and Adam said, "this is now bone of my bones..." (Genesis 2: 22, 23). We see this same principle as Jacob's wife Rachel made herself seen, as Ruth married Boaz, and even as Rahab made herself available to join to the people of God before the collapse of Jericho's walls. **Making oneself available is different from asking**.

"And let us not be weary in well-doing: for in due season we shall reap, if we faint not" Galatians 6:9

The Realities of Marriage

"If love is blind, marriage is the eye opener". I am not sure who originally stated this, but they sound like they were talking from experience. Marriage truly does open one's eyes to the truth that living with and loving someone till death do you part is not always a bed of roses. When many women dream of marriage, they picture the story of Cinderella. Do you remember Cinderella? A lady who had a really bad lot in life ends up marrying a prince and they live happily ever after. Sounds like a wonderful dream, right? But then when you wake up next to a person whom you argued with the night before about forgetting to pay the electric bill, or when you have to ask for permission about something you may have done freely a million times before, reality sets in and begins to slice… like a knife. The truth is marriage takes a lot more than money and romance. I once heard in a sermon that the word marriage is spelled W-O-R-K. In other words, it is far more than your fantasy of sweet words and expensive gifts. It is a life-time commitment to the good, the bad, and the sometimes ugliness of staying in the "fight" with the one you have chosen to love.

Have you ever wondered what makes a good marriage work? Here are some truths that I have come to embrace over the years that I believe will help put some things about marriage in perspective:

One: **You ABSOLUTELY need GOD.** Every toy comes with instructions from the manufacturer. All food comes with a list of ingredients from the company that produces it. All medicine come with warnings from the professionals that designed them. We read and heed these words as law because we trust those who developed them. So why wouldn't we seek the advice and guidance of the one who divinely designed marriage? Marriage was God's Idea. And it was a good idea. Marriage has so many wonderful benefits. However, we cannot truly experience those benefits without God being at the center. His wisdom is far more infinite, and when it comes to daily interaction with your spouse, the wisdom of God is essential. The wisdom of God is "…first pure, then peaceable, gentle, and easy to be entreated, full of mercy and good fruits, without partiality, and without hypocrisy" (James 3:17). Since God has made us autonomous beings, we are able to take action and make choices without consulting Him. However, just as the word says in John 15:5, all of those steps taken without Him end up being a lot of "nothing". In a nutshell, attempting to have a fulfilling marriage without seeking the Lord is fruitless.

From day one the enemy wants nothing more than to dismantle the union built between the two of you, brick by brick. In fact, I am convinced the moment you say "I do", spiritually your union in brandished with a bull's eye from the enemy. Just like God hates divorce (Matthew 2:16), equally the enemy hates marriage between a man and a woman. He knows that power can arise from people working together in unity with oneness of purpose and mind. The Bible says that two are better than one (Ecclesiastes 4:9-12). If a person is alone and he falls, he struggles because there is no support. But when there are two, the one will support and encourage the other "…and a three-fold cord is not quickly broken" (Ecclesiastes 4:12). There is an analogy about marriage that I learned from my spouse some years ago which I have not forgotten. It is about the "three-fold cord". The three-fold chord the scripture refers to can be pictured as the triangular relationship between you, your spouse, and God, where God is at the vertex or highpoint of the triangle. The closer the two of you draw to God, the closer you draw to each other! In addition, the more you are submitted to God, the more you are able to submit to your husband; the more you spend time in God's presence, the more you will love your wife.

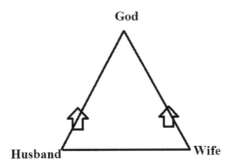

One of the most essential things you must do daily is spending time in prayer. Prayer brings such freedom and release. When I have an argument with my spouse or I am feeling frustrated with the demands of life, I stop and pray. When I do this, such a feeling of peace overwhelms me. The act of surrendering to God brings such freedom. You are no longer bearing the heavy burden of anger, disappointment, or frustration. Mathew 11:29 says "Come unto me, all ye that labour and are heavy laden, and I will give you rest". When you stop to talk to God about every aspect of your marriage, you are choosing to take His rest. By taking on His rest we also open our hearts and minds to the way He thinks. We begin to think of the situation the way our Father does, and we begin to see our spouse with His eyes. Our capacity to love and forgive also expands in that moment of surrender. We can be compassionate and become more patient with our spouse's shortcomings. This is impossible without leaning on the Father. "…Lean not unto thine own understanding. In **all** thy ways acknowledge him, and he shall surely direct thy paths" (Proverbs 3:5-6). The freedom and assurance that comes in resting and depending on God is like no other and you will experience the peace and joy that you will never know without Him. I challenge you to spend time in prayer for your spouse and your marriage. Invite God into every aspect of your marriage relationship, and you will see the positive result.

Two: **You never stop learning**. Even after 12 years of marriage there are so many lessons that I pick up daily. I have mainly learned a great deal about myself. Marriage can be a mirror for your soul. I have seen so many things in myself that I couldn't see before marriage. I remember one lesson I learned the hard way was that I was not as humble as people said I was all my life. When I found myself having to follow directives in my personal decisions, such as what I should wear or eat, I realized I had some growing to do in the humility department and it wasn't easy.

I often seek out devotionals, messages, scriptures that encourage me in my marriage and that help me learn. Instead of wasting hours of your life watching a drama series that only provides cheap entertainment, why not invest into your marriage by reading a book or watching godly videos (from reputable ministries or sources) that share on significant topics such as submission and finances in marriage. There is an unlimited supply of such videos online. All of these resources can be great tools to remind you to always seek ways to gain understanding.

Spouses should also invest time into learning from one another. For every new level in life and every new time period, your spouse will be a different person. It is important to understand this and keep an open mind to embrace them as they evolve. Be willing to re-learn them over and over again. Discover the joy of parting the layers of onion that is your spouse. The person you married is a dynamic individual, not a statue. So learn to love her more as you discover her inner workings. Learn to love every layer of his inner most contemplations. The mere fact that he trusts you enough to share more of who he is, is deeply significant, and it is an honor to be in that space with him.

Three: **You never stop growing.** In 1 Corinthians 10:12, the bible says "Wherefore let him that thinketh he standeth take heed lest he fall". Many times, in our pride, after doing something continuously, we figure that we are "masters" or "professionals" and we know exactly what we are doing. We "stand tall". The problem with standing tall on the road of life is that sometimes, as you are traveling, you reach a lower overpass that requires you to duck or get lower. If we are not observant, we are caught by surprise, knocked off our "high horse" and face the possibility

of self- inflicted injury, and negatively affect those ⸱
A couple of years into our marriage, while driving, ₁
politely told me to slow down when parking because it
an accident. In my pride, I simply told my spouse "I
driving since the age of 16. I have been driving longer
I got this"! Lo and behold, one day I was parking anc
pay attention to what I was doing and ran the car int∢
of a truck. Needless to say, that caused a heated discu
told you so" and a financial burden we did not have to
I listened and heeded the earlier warnings.

In marriage humility is key. Being humble is realizing
not have it all together on day 1 or day 4,001! I constₐ
work in progress, and I will never arrive to a place wh
growing. Knowing this reality also helps us to love oₗ
more and to have compassion. If you view them in the
growing, we will give them room for their mistakes. W
so angry at what we would consider as common sense
Just like Jesus, the one who would have every right to
faults, remembers daily that we are dust, we should reme
our spouses are fallible. "Like as a father pitieth his cₕ
the Lord pitieth them that fear him. For he knoweth ∢
he remembereth that we are dust" (Psalms 103: 13 &
spouse will make mistakes! But they are growing, anᵈ
the power to be their catalyst for growth. When I was ₚ
heard of an experiment that was conducted with plants.
wanted to see if words truly affected people, so theʸ
plant that they spoke very negatively to all the time,
had another plant whom they spoke very positively
from the words spoken to them, the plants received
same treatment (i.e. sunlight, water, temperature contrₒ
end of the experiment, to their astonishment, the planᵗ
spoken to negatively was withering and the one that wₐ
to positively was flourishing. Therefore, the gentle worᵈ
in compassion and humility to your spouse will be the ᵣ
waters they need to nourish their often weary, souls.

Four: **It Takes Everyday Effort**. As I stated before marriage is ᵥ

consistency is a significant requirement in the job description. The dictionary defines consistency as "steadfast adherence to the same principles". It also reveals the meaning as "agreement, harmony, or compatibility.". Essentially, a marriage where both husband and wife are relentlessly dedicated to the principles that make it work, will indeed experience a harmonious environment of agreement. They will thrive on great compatibility. But this doesn't just come from snapping the fingers or just hoping so. It takes everyday intentionality. Daily ACTION. This includes praying together, deliberate planning of time spent together, practicing communication, redirecting negative thoughts, studying one another and knowing each other's love language, just to name a few.

My spouse always tells me "if anything is worth doing, it's worth doing well". The problem is, naturally, we as humans can have a tendency to be lazy or feel too much at ease when things are going well. It's easy to slip into mediocrity and live life without passion. I have come to see the importance of seeking and relying on the Holy Spirit in this regard. The Holy Spirit acts as a kindle that perpetually re-ignites those embers, those remnants of passion that have died down to a meager dim glow. But the Holy Spirit is a gentleman, He will wait to be invited into your situation, He will not impose Himself. Any couple desiring to be intentional must ask the Holy Spirit daily to ignite the passion for life and their relationship, and to guide them in the right direction.

Five: **You Have to be willing to Fight the Good Fight.** What do you think of when you think of "fighting"? Two people contesting to win a victory? Rounds and rounds of "blow for blow jabs" and "ducking" and "weaving"? One smiling, decorated winner, one beatdown, defeated looser? This may be ideal for the boxing ring, but this is not the kind of fight that sustains a marriage. When you fight in marriage you have to think "we" not "me". Where there is love and you hurt each other, you are hurting yourself, because the two of you are one. The Bible says: "For no man ever yet hated his own flesh; but nourisheth and cherisheth it, even as the Lord the church" (Ephesians 5:29). Just like you make sure

you look good and you are not wanting for anything, you do the same for your spouse. You cherish them and value the position God has placed you within their life. Anyone that struggles with loving and cherishing their spouse must first look at the love they have for God.

ISo, if not fighting in the traditional or physical sense, what kind of fighting are we talking about here? "Fight the good fight of Faith, lay hold on eternal life, whereunto thou art also called, and hast professed a good profession before many witnesses" (1 Timothy 6:12). Have you ever seen an Olympic long-distance track race? There have been many instances when I watched a race like this, and it comes down to the wire. Two runners are "neck and neck" and they are intensely giving it all they have got. You can literally see the veins popping out from their neck as they are rigidly flexing their muscles and pumping their arms; propelling themselves forward with a fire in their eyes that says "I …will …win… this one!" They have decided that they will fight with all they have got to attain the prize they have trained for and endured for. Yes, they may be tired, it has been a long journey, but even in the final strides they refuse to relent. They push forward with greater intensity because they have chosen to fight a good fight to the very end. In this regard, the fight in marriage is like a marathon, a fight of endurance; but at the same time, it is a relay where we partner with our spouse. In other words, you and your spouse are not each other's enemies! The enemy of your marriage is principally, the devil. Therefore, the fight is against the devil and we need to partner with our spouse everyday in prayer, submission, love and the word of God to win this battle. "For we wrestle not against flesh and blood, but against principalities, against powers, against the rulers of the darkness of this world, against spiritual wickedness in high places" (Ephesians 6:12).

Six: **Quitting is Not an Option.** If you were told one day that you would be given $100 million dollars if you walked one-hundred miles, would you do it? Most people would say absolutely! What if you got tired at the 30-mile mark? Would you stop? What if at the 50-mile mark it started to rain? Would you give up? What if your shoe broke at the 95-mile mark? Would you still keep going? I think even through all of those obstacles, that money would be very enticing to you and the hope of obtaining it definitely would encourage perseverance. Your eyes would always be on the prize and not the temporary circumstance. I'm tired, but I am almost to the end and I can buy a new car. It's raining, but I am halfway to buying an unlimited amount of umbrellas. My shoe broke, ha! But I am 5 miles to 100 brand new pairs of shoes. You see it is all about *perspective*. Not focusing on the present, but knowing that God has completed the ending even before the beginning (Is. 46:10). No matter how difficult it can be, I must refuse to be selfish and love you when I get angry, annoyed, frustrated, or hurt. Despite the fact that we are struggling to pay the bills and buy food at the moment, I see us travelling the world together after we have said goodbye to our cooperate jobs. Even though, you said something to me in a moment of anger that cut deep, I see us sitting on the porch in our rocking chairs enjoying the sunset in our old age. Even though we are desperate to conceive now, and it is bringing such sorrow, I see us blissfully playing hide-and -seek with our grandchildren when they come spend time with us during the summers.

Seven: **It's not about ME.** In a world full of rejection, where your spouse can sometimes feel beaten down at every turn, they need your acceptance and support. It gives that person life when you show them unconditional acceptance and love, in spite of their imperfections and mistakes. When you do that you are loving them like Jesus. They will see the light of Christ in you and be drawn to Him more because of your love. I know… I know, but they leave their socks in the wrong places, and they nag too much, and they never get the right things on the grocery list, or they do not remember important dates, or they are forever breaking or losing things! This is how Jesus loves us, in spite of ourselves. This is the place where we go beyond ME. Your focus should not always be on yourself but the wellbeing of your spouse as well. Remember, **J**esus first, **O**thers next, and **Y**ourself last is the key to joy in marriage! Another thing to consider is the importance of what we call "reflective happiness" in marriage and with one's kids.

Reflective happiness is doing something for someone that does not benefit you in any way other than the happiness you gain from seeing the person being happy. An example of reflective happiness is Jesus dying on the cross for us and his joy about our salvation

A pastor (Pastor Dennis Rouse) once said: **"If you want to be closer to Jesus stay single; if you want to be more like Jesus, get married"**. What does this mean? People who are single have more personal time to spend with God and therefore, have more opportunity to be closer to God. "He that is unmarried careth for the things that belong to the Lord, how he may please the Lord" (1 Corinthians 7:32). On the other hand, people who are married have more opportunities to be selfless like Jesus on a daily basis. "But he that is married careth for the things that are of the world, how he may please his wife" (1 Corinthians 7:33). From the Bible, we see that while on Earth, Jesus lived a life of selflessness. He was a servant to all. He walked in complete humility. He was King, yet he voluntarily washed people's withered, dirty feet, without complaint (John 13). In this light, marriage opens your world to a life beyond singleness and self. Before you walk down the aisle, your main activities and concerns in life generally center around you. But once you say "I do" you pledge to dedicate your life in the service of your spouse. You have been placed in their life to make a positive impact on their destiny. Even if it is as simple as making a meal or helping them get out of the car after a long day at work, the effects of your intentional acts of service are immeasurable; and when you serve them, you are serving God (Galatians 5:13).

I was having a conversation with one of my single friends the other day. We were analyzing a list that had been forwarded concerning do's and don'ts for good wives. After looking at some statements regarding not being confrontational and changing some behaviors to appease your husband, she shared that she was okay with the idea of marriage, but she did not want to lose her identity or voice in it. I contemplated this for a moment, because it seemed like a very valid point. Typical women in the western world are heavily influenced by the 20th Century social movement of feminism. Society has developed the ideal of the "independent woman." Women are taught to be, self-reliant, strong individuals, who do not need men. After thinking, God placed something in my heart to share with her. One of the key purposes of marriage is to lose "self". <u>When you submit to God you are surrendering who you think you are to become EVERYTHING He wants you to be</u>. **For a marriage to be successful you need to take off "you" and put on Him (God).** Isaiah 55:9 says: "…my ways are higher than your ways, and my thoughts than your thoughts". If you try to hold on to your voice, your way of doing things, you will utterly fail at marriage. But to produce something beautiful, you must be that seed that dies in the ground, shedding off the old. Jesus, who is God, understood and demonstrated this type of humility when He came to Earth as a human being. Philippians 2 says that when He came, He didn't cling to the fact that He was equal to God, but humbly submitted to be reduced to human form. He was innocent, yet He offered himself to die a criminal's death. Now, if Jesus could do these things as our ultimate example, then we must do the same and we will see the same rewards of promotion and living a life emptied of ourselves.

Wives were created to help their husbands. God said that he would make Adam "a help meet for him" (Genesis 2:18). The creation of Eve, then signified that Adam needed help and she was exactly the tailored made help he needed. The role of a wife as helper is vital. The purpose and destiny given to the husband and ultimately to the family cannot be realized without the support and help of the wife. Once she connects to her husband, she divinely becomes an integral instrument in his life orchestra. Have you ever heard an orchestra where everybody played their own song? In two words….. TOTAL CHAOS! Yet, there is a beautiful melody that brings such peace and serenity when instruments play in unison. In other words, when a wife aligns with the vision and purpose of the husband, she walks in agreement and enables him to daily pursue and carry out with relative ease, the will of God for his life. This requires that she doesn't seek her own agenda. This is not to say a wife cannot have desires or passions, but if these pursuits do not ultimately support her husband and the overall vision of the family, it is against the will of God. If a wife's career pursuit causes her family to suffer, then it is time to re-evaluate. In Proverbs 31, God outlines and highlights the character and role of a wife after God's heart. All that she does, strengthens and protects her family and her home, and promotes her husband as a leader among leaders. Her husband trusts her to run the home as he is conducting business outside the home, because she daily works diligently and with great detail to orchestrate all activities of her home and makes sure things run smoothly (Prov. 31:11). Her tireless dedication to the betterment of her family does not make her a weak woman without identity and wasted degrees, as society now promotes. On the contrary, at the end of her selflessness, her name is made great: "Many daughters have done virtuously, but thou excellest them all" (Proverbs 31:29). Wives must pursue the loss of self and selfish agendas, and surrender wholly to the Father by submitting to His will and submitting to our own husbands as unto the Lord. "Wives submit yourselves unto your own husbands, as unto the Lord" (Ephesians 5:22). This is hard to do! I will never pretend that it is easy. How do I know? Because I have the battle scars to prove it. Who have I been fighting with? Myself! My flesh. Like Jacob, many of us wrestle through the "night" times (Genesis 32:24-28) to shed the old ways and to be more like Him; to transform from Jacob to Israel. This process totally takes the resolve to want more than YOUR SELF. The kind of dig your fingernails in the dirt tenacity to go beyond me and want more of Him. It is an everyday effort. Though I fall, I WILL NOT GIVE UP!

Have you ever been kayaking? Paddling on the water in a narrow vessel can be thrilling, challenging, and a bit scary to a novice. The other day I was kayaking with my spouse for the first time. There we were, fully clothed (can you tell we were newbies?), suited in life jackets, trudging in calf-high water to get to a kayak waiting for us on the beach. I sat in the front and my spouse sat in the back. We struggled for a while to get our bearings and to understand how it "all" worked, but we were having fun on our new adventure. My spouse is really good at assessing situations and developing plans of action to best navigate us through challenges. I am good at staying calm in periods of high stress, but my problem is I often want to lead when I should follow. Based on their assessment, my spouse decided we should paddle in a certain way and go in a particular direction. I, on the other hand, had my own ideas because I wanted to act out what I saw on t.v. Interestingly enough, in kayaking the person sitting at the back should be the one to steer, and the one in front sets the pace. The problem came when we both tried to paddle with no single direction. We were not paddling in harmony or on one accord. We kept going in circles and eventually ended up stuck in the sand on the beach (twice). My unwillingness to yield turned what was to be a fun activity into an arduous journey. God showed me that in the same way, this is what happens in many marriages. When you do not submit to the leadership of your home, you end up going in the same circle again and getting "stuck". It takes wisdom and the strength of God to be honest with yourself and surrender. If you are seeing patterns of vicious relationship killing cycles in your marriage, I challenge you to examine yourself. Ask the Father to reveal your heart to you. Let Him show you the area you may not have submitted to Him yet, in order that He might break the cycle and set your marriage free.

Eight: **One of the most powerful phrases in marriage is "I'm sorry".** You and your wife are at a dinner with some friends. You, feeling in a jovial mood, decide to share with everyone about how your wife was such a bad cook when you two first got married that she even burned boiled eggs. Admittedly, the story is quite amusing, and everyone has a hearty laugh…. everyone, except your wife. You catch a glimpse of her mouth tightly spread into a polite plastic smile and notice she is seemingly turning red with embarrassment or is it anger? For your sake, you are praying it is not the latter. After leaving dinner you notice that you are getting the silent treatment on the ride home. Although you already know the answer you decide to ask: "Honey what's wrong"? After a few minutes of prodding, your wife erupts into an emotional rant about you being very inconsiderate and her feeling completely humiliated. Initially, within you, your first response is "Why are you being so sensitive? It was the truth. You are overreacting. You have shared embarrassing memories about me, and I have never reacted this way"! After contemplating for a moment, you decide not to go with your initial instincts, but consider this woman next to you whom you have chosen to love through ups and downs and inspite of imperfections. You empathetically key into her pain and realize your actions genuinely hurt her and possibly rubbed some salt into the wounds of insecurity that still needs more time to heal. Realizing your mistake, you wholeheartedly say those two little words that her heart needs to hear: "I'm sorry".

"I'm sorry": two little words with often big results. This simple phrase is a mighty weapon against offense, it can calm the biggest storm, and put out many fires! When you apologize for wrongdoing or offenses, you validate your spouse's concerns. You acknowledge their feelings and make them feel and know that you value them. It also builds layers of trust because your spouse sees that you are not just out for your own gain, to always prove you are right. It shows love because it takes love to be humble enough to admit wrongdoing. And it truly takes the grace of God to be wrong even when you are right. I have seen time and time again the negative effects of trying to prove I am right versus humbling myself to be wrong for the sake of peace. People often find this difficult because of the risk of appearing weak. On the contrary it takes far more strength to admit mistakes or to forsake your ego, especially when you **know** you are right. In the end, it is never good to force your way and win the battle, because you might ultimately loose the war.

Nine: **Trust is a BIG deal.** It takes a lot of guts and work to truly be our authentic selves. When I say "work", I mean it is far less effort to be a counterfeit. People are easily fake. Just look at some people who flash you that "quick- reflex- and -drop-smile" when you glance their way. FAKE! It takes far more selflessness to want to brighten someone else's day with a warm greeting when your eyes meet, not knowing how they will respond. So, most people rather just live life as an imitation of themselves because it is easier and less risky. However, in Christ-centered marriages, authenticity has to be at the core. Each spouse is willing to share the deepest parts of themselves to become connected in unity with their husband or wife. This takes a lot of courage and trust becomes a major factor.

For men trusting their wife with who they are, their dreams, and aspirations, is a major leap. Can I trust you with my secrets? Most men rather be private successes than public failures, so they live a good portion of their single life guarded. In other words, a man may not let most people know that they are starting a business (just mainly business partners), they would just share the good news of the success once it has taken off. Therefore, once he takes that courageous step to be vulnerable with his wife, a man is in expectation to have a confidant who is truly for him and who will be his biggest support. Proverbs 31:11 says that: "the heart of the husband doth safely trust in her". The Amplified version takes it a step further and says: "the heart of her husband trusts in her confidently _and_ relies on and believes in her securely". This means he feels safe with her. He is assured that she will act in his best interest and always be a good support.

For women trust is a matter of action. Can I trust you to provide, protect, and care for me? Can I trust you with my heart? This is essential especially for women who have experienced heartbreak and disappointments in previous relationships. They often live with the fear of rejection and rather just remain guarded than allow someone the chance to possibly hurt them again. So, a wife wants a relationship she also feels secure in. This requires deliberate actions on the part of the husband. What a husband does and what a husband says are two different things. Though you may say "I love you" if you don't show affection or if you also speak harshly all the time, or if you do not make time for her, she may not really believe your professions.

When trust is broken in a marriage whether it be a simple lie or something as life altering as adultery, it is an intricate process involved in building it once again. Though the couple can quickly resolve to stay united and forgive one another, trust takes time. For that husband or wife who has been the spouse of the adulterer, their period of healing may take time, and some may even experience phases of grieving while coming to terms with what has happened. For both parties, it is essential to be patient with one another and fight to rebuild the connection that was breached, and rebuild the bridge of trust that will bring you two together again.

CHAPTER 2

BECOMING THE PARENT GOD INTENDED FOR MY CHILDREN)

"Lo children are an heritage of the Lord: and the fruit of the womb is his reward. As arrows are in the hand of a mighty man: so are children of the youth. Happy is the man that hath his quiver full of them ..." Psalm 27:3-5

g as a Family

,
many people, after getting married, the next step is "starting a
As sensible as this sounds, I think there is an error that needs to be
. When a man and a woman come together in a marriage union,
already a family. When you have children, you are expanding
ily unit. In essence, you are adding another floor to an already
house, with a firm foundation. Having the mindset that you are
ily until you have children can stunt the growth of your union
ten its solidarity. Before the kids its "You and I". After the kids

---

"Then came Peter to him, and said, Lord, how oft shall my brother sin against me, and I forgive him? till seven times? Jesus saith unto him, I say not unto thee, Until seven times: but, Until seventy times seven". Matthew 18:21-22

Becoming the Forgiver God Intended for my Spouse

"Marriage is two forgivers living together". Words spoken by a wise woman of faith (the late Pastor Bimbo Odukoya). I have come to see how true these words are. The bible says that offenses will come (Matthew 18:7). This is especially true in marriage. When two people merge to become one, it is a sometimes-painful process. **Forgivers are a blessing because they give out the unmerited blessing of forgiveness like Christ did on the cross**. Forgiveness is a requirement in marriage because of the imperfect nature of man. Reinhard Bohnke said: **"the perfect marriage requires a perfect husband and a perfect wife. A perfect husband is the one who does not expect his wife to be perfect; and the perfect wife is the one who does not expect her husband to be perfect; but both have a perfect savior – Jesus"**!

In the book of Hosea in the Bible, there is a story about Hosea and Gomer, a very unlikely couple who learned a very hard lesson in forgiveness. You see, Hosea was a man of God and Gomer was a prostitute. Despite their massive differences, Hosea marries Gomer and takes her from a life of whoredom to a completely different existence where she is now valued as a human being, and cherished as a wife and mother. However, the days of bliss are short-lived when Gomer abruptly returns to her former ways and comes home pregnant by another man. As if that isn't enough, after experiencing this gut wrenching and I am sure humiliating ordeal, Hosea is asked again by God to take his wife in and purchase her freedom. So once again Hosea claims her as his own and declares with authority "thou shalt not be for another man". (Hosea 3:3) This amazing story clearly displays love and forgiveness in its purest form. Hosea loved his wife just as the bible commanded despite her sins and shortcomings. "Husbands, love your wives, even as Christ also loved the church, and gave himself for it. That he might sanctify and cleanse it with the washing of water by the word. …So ought men to love their wives as their own bodies. He that loveth his wife loveth himself" (Galatians 5:25, 26). The love of the husband for the wife is God's divinely designed replication of His love relationship with us, the church. God commands the husband to love the wife, the way he loves us – unconditionally. He does this so that we can have a glimpse of His infinite love for us. He loves us so much that he would forgive and take us in over and over again as Hosea did. Hosea's love redeemed Gomer from her former life. He gave her worth.

What if we were like Jesus the ultimate forgiver; always standing ready to forgive the sins or transgressions of our spouse past, present and future. The weight of offense would be virtually non-existent. Jesus our ultimate forgiver is our supreme example. We are only able to live the life of a forgiver in Him. It is impossible to do it in and of ourselves. The Bible says that God removes our sin from us as far as the East is from the West (Psalms 103:12). Imagine if we were to forgive like that.

Just as God commands the husband to love (Ephesians 5:25), He commands the wife to submit (Ephesians 5:22). Now why would he command such a hard thing? How does a woman who is used to being autonomous and making her own decisions now go back to getting permission or accept when she can't do as she pleases? How does she surrender her will and say yes to his? Perhaps God divinely designed and assigned these roles to exemplify His relationship with us. God loves us completely, in spite of ourselves and despite the fact that we do not always show we love Him. His love is unconditional. In the same light He expects that we as His bride would give ourselves over to Him, surrender our will to Him. Follow after Him in love and faith, even when we don't agree or understand. When a husband and wife live out this dynamic in front of their children, the children learn about the nature of God and they also learn how they should handle their relationship with God.

When all is said and done, and your spouse has gone to be with God, you won't have need to complain about the make up smudges on the mirror or the socks left on the floor. In fact, you will long for those things again. Your heart will long for the imperfections you at times loathed before. You only have one chance, one opportunity on earth to love that person the way God intended and after that, it's gone. Cherish every moment. Be patient. Be kind. Forgive quickly. Love wholeheartedly. Love unconditionally.

"Set your affection on things abo[ve]
things on the earth" Colossian[s]

Preparing Together on Earth for Eternity

Marriage is not just about focus on earth [and having] children, raising kids, having grandkids, payin[g for] houses, buying cars, making wills, saving for reti[rement] and other things we value. It should be focused on [Colossians 3:2]. Things such as how to ensure our kids are go[ing to Heaven,] ensure our grandkids have the legacy of Christ, [things] such as passing out tracks at the mall, family alt[ar, praying] for each other, and much more. Furthermore, e[ach should] be better spiritually as a result of the marriage. [The] spouse should not be derailed after marriage b[ut grow as] days go by. "Iron sharpeneth iron; so a man sh[arpeneth the countenance] of his friend" (Proverbs 27:17)

There are many dynamics within the relati[onship of a husband] and a wife. Spouses can be best friends, busin[ess partners,] laborers, and even co-workers. Spiritually speak[ing, the husband is the priest] of the home and there are also times when the [husband operates as] the prophet. Equally, the wife can operate as a [prophetess but] the two of you must work together to understan[d the various] roles that define your unity. There is no marri[age in Heaven but] even beyond husbands and wives, one of the m[ost important roles is] brothers and sisters in Christ. The husband al[so is the priest] of the family and the wife should submit to h[im] because that's the first church of the family.

Grow[ing]

To [raise a godly] family". [Children should be] correcte[d] they are[?] your fa[mily] standin[g] not a fa[mily] and thre[e]

have gone into families of their own it will be "You and I". Nothing comes between "us". It is important to make a commitment with one another not to abandon or neglect your roles as husband and wife as the children come. You are her husband first before you are "Princess's" dad, and you are his wife first before you are little "Junior's" mom. This requires a great deal of intentionality because as the kids come with their needs, it can be a very big temptation to center everything around them (this is especially true for mothers). You never want your spouse to feel as if they are being replaced or are in a competition for your time and affection. Abraham and Sarah as well as Isaac and Rebekah understood the importance of cultivating their relationship with one another while awaiting the expansion their family. They exemplified a close bond. Sarah honored and submitted to her husband to the extent of calling him "lord" (1 Peter 3:6). Isaac and Rebekah were so loving and affectionate with one another so much so that the King took notice (Genesis 26:8). It takes the grace of God to balance the many roles that evolve as your family grows, but I know our God will cause you to excel in Jesus' name!

If the natural next step after getting married is having children, what happens when there is a delay? Don't worry, there is hope in God. Psalms 62:8 declares: "Trust in him at all times; ye people, pour out your heart before him: God is a refuge for us. Selah". Remember Hannah, the mother of Samuel the Prophet, poured out her heart before God about this same issue; and God heard and answered her (1 Samuel 1). Some other biblical examples for trusting God for the fruit of the womb are Zacharias and Elizabeth; Abraham and Sarah; Isaac and Rebekah; Jacob and Rachel; Samson's parents, etc. **All these babies (Samson, Isaac, Jacob, Joseph, John the Baptist, etc.) that were born out of waiting patiently on God, turn out to be very important world changers, and they left their mark permanently on history**. Be encouraged in your wait and know that your seed that is coming through your line, is a world changer, and God is preparing you for your blessing like he got Abraham ready for Isaac! Remember, Psalms 127:3 declares: "Lo, children are an heritage of the LORD: <u>and the fruit of the womb is his reward</u>".

"♪ Hush little arrow don't say a word...... ♪". In Psalm 127:4, our heavenly father uses the analogy of an archer and an arrow to describe the intricacy involved in the parent-child dynamic. He says that our children are like arrows in our hands and we are blessed when we have many of them. The other day, I was reading the steps an archer has to take to launch an arrow toward a target. First the archer must aim the bow down toward the ground, then load the arrow onto the bow. And I likened bending that bow to submitting myself as a parent to the will of God. Getting on my knees and seeking the face of God in order to get wisdom to direct my children in the right way and down the right path. Once the archer places the arrow onto the bow, he has to point the arrow and bow upwards before setting aim at his target. I liken this to introducing our children to Christ and teaching them the ways of God, which is the first step in aiming them in the right direction. Now, the task of pulling on that bow string and stretching the arrow back into position, ready to launch, is not quick and easy. But it takes a steady hand, consistency, and dedication, and a willingness to be committed and intentional to direct that child to the right target. It takes strength – the strength that only comes from God. You are aiming that child into their destiny. As a parent you have a very vital role because an arrow that is launched aimlessly, can be lethal. It can destroy lives and can cause irreparable damage. But an arrow that is launched with intentionality will hit the target and bring reward, and a feeling of accomplishment and success. Children are your arrows, your weapons against the adversary; to defeat the kingdom of darkness: to destroy the works of the devil. Each one of those babies are significant. Anyone aimed in the right way can make a huge impact and change the world! There are many examples of the damage caused by misusing our God-given arrows. I knew a child that always stole things from other kids; and his mom sat idly by and made excuses for his improper actions. When the boy became a man, he of course had become more skillful in the act of stealing and defrauding others. This led to severe legal troubles that embarrassed the parents.

As the family grows, remember that each child is different and uniquely so. "I will praise thee; for I am fearfully and wonderfully made: marvellous are thy works; and that my soul knoweth right well" (Psalm 139:14). Therefore, each child's uniqueness should be accounted for and celebrated. Also, dare to parent differently than the way the world does. As your child is unique, be a unique parent as well. The word (of God) is your yardstick not the world!

"For unto us a child is born...." Isaiah 9:6

The Joy of the First Child – Planting Season

From the moment you hear the words "you are having a baby", a flood of emotions and great joy captures your heart; and your life and family are forever changed! During pregnancy, every stage of growth fills your heart with great expectation as you await the new arrival. You begin looking for a name for the child, going for routine medical checks, hearing the baby's heartbeat, feeling the baby's kicks and movements, and buying baby clothes and furniture. Once your little one joins the family and you become a trio (or more in the case of twins, etc.), your daily life becomes filled with firsts. You start awaiting the baby's first smile, first rollover, first steps, first words, first day at school, the list can go on for years to include graduation, 1st job, marriage, and they themselves finally becoming parents! The birth of the very first child into a family is always a thing of joy. When parents have their first child, there is immediately a big change in the family dynamics. First comes uncontrolled joy and amazement at the beauty that is beheld – the baby! Then comes the perhaps unexpected lessons of practical parenthood which includes some sleepless nights (in some cases) due to the baby needing so much attention. That shift of attention to the baby's need is the beginning of hard work that is needed to keep the joy of parenthood even when they become an adult. With all these God orchestrated events, there is no reason not to treasure family!

Have you ever watched a farmer at work? The life of a farmer is definitely not easy but can be very rewarding when one reaps the fruits of their labor. As parents we are divinely appointed farmers for the better part of the first 20 years or so of our children's lives. We can call this planting season. During planting season, farmers spend countless hours surveying the land, tilling the land to prepare it for seeds, planting the seeds, watering the seeds, removing weeds, guarding against pest invaders, and ensuring proper exposure to the sun. As diligent "farmers", we work to develop our children as instruments in the Master's hand. We cultivate our home as protective environment where our children have the freedom to grow and learn. We provide them with the physical, spiritual, and emotional nourishment they need to flourish. We protect their innocence from evil influence and infiltration; and guard them against the limits of society and the enemy that would inhibit their destiny.

During the planting season, it is important to build solid relationships with our children. From the beginning, human beings were made for relationship. God himself refers to himself as "Father", identifying himself through relationship. He interacts with us his children, as a loving Father wanting to have a close relationship with us. When parents do not have a solid relationship with their children, they are more apt to only see their children's faults. They are less forgiving. The bond of relationship is powerful. When we as parents seek to truly **know** our children and love them for who they are, then we can fully appreciate the way God made them. They in turn feel a sense of belonging. They know they are a part of something greater than themselves. They thrive in that soil. Our solid family relationship is the soil from which our children grow, thrive and become mighty oaks and plantings of our God (Isaiah 61:3). We as "farmer" parents, must do all we can to make sure that the soil is fertile, to make sure that we water them with the washing of the word, and to make sure we place them in the sun (the Son of God).

"And the child grew, and waxed strong in spirit, filled with wisdom: and the grace of God was upon him" Luke 2:40. "

Dealing with Teenage Children

Arguably, one of the most famous set of parents in history would be Mary the mother of Jesus and Joseph, his earthly father. These two were ordinary people yet anointed by God to help in the upbringing of the Savior of the world. What a task! I wonder what they must have felt that fateful day when Jesus was born. Did they feel they would be up to the challenge? I know if it were me, I might feel a bit intimidated and even unworthy. As a parent of a teenage child, you might also feel unsure and inadequate, but yet God has chosen you to love and to train His perfect gift that would ultimately impact the world for His glory. However, there are some things to consider. The Bible depicts an incident that arose during Jesus' youth (Luke 2:41-48). You see, Mary and Joseph travelled to Jerusalem every year, according to the customs of Passover. They did so also the year Jesus turned twelve. Once the festivities were done, the Bible says Mary and Joseph assumed that Jesus was with them and kept going about their daily lives. In fact, they went a whole day's journey before they began to look for Him. This narrative teaches us four important things as parents.

Number one: Never get so busy with living your daily life that you leave your teenage child behind. We as adults often get caught in a "rat race" where we spend a lot of time trying to amass things and meet goals at the expense of being with our kids. Jesus was a different case because he was so hungry for God that all he wanted was to learn more about God form the synagogue. Many teenage children today, will fill the void caused by the neglect of their parents with negative peer influence, the foolishness of the world and the lusts thereof. Your "teenager" is still a child and should be considered a teenage child, rather than a "teenager". The connotation of the term "teenager" psychologically makes us as parents feel they are grown and independent, needing little or no more parental attention, supervision or guidance. However, when you view your "teenager" as a teenage child, you will always remember that a child is still a child, and a child still requires a great deal of parental influence. Even though there is reduced parental influence at this stage, it should still be there.

Number two: Though independence is good, as a parent, do not be in a rush for them to grow up. Jesus' parents may have given him his independence pre-maturely (by allowing him to roam freely) before it dawned on them that they had made a mistake. Though it is challenging and it requires a lot of sacrifice and investment from you, it is best to enjoy every stage of the child's development, releasing them to their full independence at the appropriate time. For example, my second daughter (who was the youngest child) was not yet ready to walk, but I felt I wanted to be done with the baby stage of parenting. So, in an effort to speed up the process of her growth and independence, I put pressure on her daily to walk. I focused so much on her walking that I don't even remember now how she crawled, and I did not enjoy that stage of her life. When we rush them, we can miss out on even the little things. From the moment your child is born, they are in a perpetual motion towards independence and even leaving you. "Therefore, shall a man leave his father and his mother, and shall cleave unto his wife: and they shall be one flesh" (Genesis 2:24). "For this cause shall a man leave his father and mother, and cleave to his wife" (Mark 10:7). When the bible speaks about a man (or woman) leaving his (or her) father and mother to cleave to their wife (or husband), it is not an instant event. The leaving is a gradual transformation of the relationship that should reach a point of celebrated accomplishment and a pinnacle of release during their wedding. Therefore, focus on, and cherish every moment that God gives you with them.

Number three: While it is important to not rush our kids to grow or be independent, it is equally important to ensure we do not hinder their growth and maturity by perpetually "babying" our kids. Sometimes, out of fear, we can be very over-protective and over-bearing when it comes to our kids. <u>We therefore need godly wisdom and the guidance of God in balancing between rushing our kids to growing, and being too over protective of them.</u> Over-protectiveness could cause rebellion in the future. *If you cover a plant, it will not grow!*

Number four: When it comes to your teenage child, never **assume** that Jesus is there. Daily disciple your children. From a young age, <u>introduce them to the word of God and the God of the word!</u> They will not get far only knowing the God of their parents, they must know Him personally. This should be your topmost desire (and prayer) for your children: "That I might know him, and the power of his resurrection, and the fellowship of his sufferings, being made conformable unto his death" (Philippians 3:10).

Number five: Never get so busy with living your daily life that you leave Jesus behind. He should be the center of all that you do and all that you are as a parent. If you do stray and follow a path where Jesus is not walking with you, the only way to correct it, is to retrace your steps and go back to the place where you abandoned His leading. This can be a long and emotional trek back, but it is necessary in order to train children who fulfill the will of God for their life.

"And the child grew, and waxed strong in spirit, and was in the desserts till the day of his showing unto Israel" Luke 1:80.

The Transition of Kids to Adults

In the transition of kids to adults:

One: **Have a vision for your child**. In having a vision for your child, what you see is what you get (Genesis 13:14-16)! God told Abraham "…look now toward heaven, and tell the stars, if thou be able to number them: and he said unto him, so shall thy seed be" (Genesis 15:5). A major part of parenting is perception. How do you see your role as a parent? How do you see your child or children? If you can only see them for who they are today, they will never reach greatness tomorrow. In the book of Hebrews 11:23-26, Paul reflects on two people who had the faith to see the hand of God on their child's life: the parents of Moses. Significantly, it says in Hebrews 11:23 (Amplified Version): "By faith Moses, after his birth, was hidden for three months by his parents, because they <u>saw</u> he was a beautiful and divinely favored child; and they were not afraid of the king's decree". In other words, Moses' parents were discerning, and they were intentional. They <u>saw</u> the destiny on his life and protected it. They hid him from the dangers and snares of the world. They provide him a covering, solace, and peace in the midst of the all the turmoil swirling around them. Their home was a safe haven where he could grow strong enough to live out his purpose. And they were not concerned with the demands of society. They didn't follow popular opinion. They followed the vision God placed in front of them for their little one and pursued purpose. When it was time to release Moses out into the world, he was encapsulated in the fortified "basket" of a strong foundation or beginning. In turn, Moses evolving from this foundation, was able to stand in faith, and refuse the life of luxury and sin that Egypt had to offer. He preferred to follow the path of light affliction (2 Corinthians 4:17) attached to walking in God's will. We as parents must provide the covering and environment our children need to thrive and grow strong in the Lord. This time that they are under our roof is a time to provide a solid foundation, a strong beginning, where they develop values and understanding of their true identity in Jesus. It is important to always remember that the teenage years of our children is their final transition from kids to adults. As such, that might be our last opportunity to mold or shape them to what God wants them to be, as well as our last chance to correct any behavior, attitude or trait that needs correction.

Two: **Speak life over your children**. Despite how seemingly dismal the present may look, see them in their future – the way God sees them. Allow God to speak over them through you. In Luke 1, we see that God sealed the mouth of Zacharias when he began to speak negatively concerning the prophesy of the birth of his son John the Baptist. Zacharias later realized the power of his tongue and chose to submit to God's will in giving his son a name. This act of obedience caused his speech to be restored and he then prophesied over his son John the Baptist (Luke 1:68-69). Your child's future is in your mouth. "Death and life are in the power of the tongue: and they that live it shall eat the fruit thereof" (Proverbs 18:21). You have the power to create or utterly destroy your children with your words. Furthermore, you are His representative to your precious little ones. When they look at you, they see God. Therefore, submit yourself to act as our Heavenly Father would want you to act in your children's lives. Draw them closer when they make mistakes and they repent, by telling them words of affirmation. In addition to words, always assure them of your love through your actions. Show compassion and mercy. Be humble by <u>saying</u> you are sorry when you are wrong [be humble also by allowing them to teach you and correct you (Isaiah. 66:2, Matthew 23.12)]. Kids should be able to <u>respectfully and appropriately</u> address imperfections of parents at any age.

Also, like Zacharias seek God's heart when naming your child. There is power in names, for example: Jesus – Isaiah 9:6; John the Baptist – Luke

1:60-63; Benjamin – Genesis 35:18; Jabez – 1 Chronicles 4:9; Israel (Jacob) – Genesis 32:28; Abraham (Abram) – Genesis 17:5; Sara (Sara) – (Genesis 17:50). God highlights the importance of names through the correction He brought in the naming of Benjamin. In Rachel's agony as she is dying, she names her newborn son Ben-oni, which means "son of my sorrow". Jacob, being discerning and prompted by the leading of God, changes his name to Benjamin "son of my right hand". Jacob knew bearing that first name would curse his son's life. Therefore, speaking into our children's lives starts even with the names we give to them.

Three: **Lead a house of disciples**. Did you know your children are your disciples? As parents we have disciples that we have the privilege of leading from birth. And just as Paul said in 1 Corinthians 11:1, our kids should follow us as we follow Christ. Jesus commissions us as believers in Matthew 28:19-20 to go out into every nation and teach others about Him and His ways and commandments. This process first starts at home. Parents are commissioned to establish the nations in their home first. Each child is a precious gift and a new nation of the world in seed form. What a privilege we as parents have to disciple our children and to win them for the Lord. Teaching children to be courageous and confident in Christ is important in establishing identity. A child who has courage will not back down from challenges. A child who understand and believes in the power of Christ on the inside of them, they will choose faith over fear. Like a solid wood chair supports the weight of a person with a large frame, children who have their identity hid in Christ feel stability and are empowered to be who God has created them to be. "Train up a child in the way he should go: and when he is old, he will not depart from it" (Proverbs 22:6). They are our mission field.

In leading a house of disciples, discipline is a part of discipleship. Discipline helps combat dysfunctions that can carry over to adulthood. Not only is discipline important, but the use of the rod of correction is very biblical. "Foolishness is bound in the heart of a child; but the rod of correction shall drive it far from him" (Proverbs 22:15). In disciplining kids and/or using the rod of correction, let us be careful not to cross over to any form of child abuse. There can be a thin line between forms of discipline, and child abuse. Even the bible says: "And, ye fathers, provoke not your children to wrath: but bring them up in the nurture and admonition of the Lord" (Ephesians 6:4); and "Fathers, provoke not your children to anger, lest they be discouraged" (Colossians 3:21). Whilst the bible admonishes us to use the rod of correction to discipline our kids, he warns us not to provoke them to wrath because they are emotional beings. There have been cases of parents trying to discipline their kids and end up severely hurting them physically causing permanent damage to their bodies or in some cases, killing their kids. Even though that may not be the intention, the actions were permanent or fatal. Therefore, an important key to disciplining kids is to do it in love, and not in anger. There has to be the right balance between our general display of love, and our display of love through the use of the rod of correction. Some children have been so abused by their parents (in the process of discipline) that the kids who are now adults, do not believe in disciplining their own kids because of the years of scars, hurts and abuse that they suffered from their own parents. I was in a bible conference on parenting when a hurting man discussed the grief he had towards his father's abuse to him as a child. As a result of this, he does not believe in the use of the rod of correction at all. Even some societies have laws that make it a crime for a parent to use the rod of correction on their children because many have abused their children. The simple truth to this is that even though others may abuse what God intended for correction in love, it does not negate God's word on the importance of the rod of correction in training our kids. Some analogies that comes to mind is that of the rich man and Lazarus (Luke 16:19-31). God's word says for us to give and it shall be given to us good measure… (Luke 6 38). This rich man was doing the opposite – being very stingy towards Lazarus the beggar, yet the rich man had in surplus. Does this negate the word of God on giving? Certainly not! Also, society has so changed now to allow homosexual marriages as legal, while God's words teaches us that marriage is between a man and a woman (Genesis 2:24, Romans 1:26-28). The abuse of marriage by society, law makers and government should not cause a firm believer to doubt God's word on the basic principle of marriage. **What others do to abuse God's word and principles does not change God's commands or instructions to us.** Hebrews 12:6 declares: "For whom the Lord loveth he chasteneth, and scourgeth every son whom he receiveth". Proverbs 3:12 says: "For whom the Lord loveth he correcteth; even as a father the son in whom he delighted".

With regards to discipline, discipline begets discipline. In other words, when we as parents are disciplined, it is easier to translate that discipline in our lives, to the lives of our offspring. This is because, they will not only hear you "talk the talk" (say things), but they will also see you "walk the walk" (do things). The crime of a parent is not making mistakes, but making mistakes and not being able to apologize and/or make amends. When our children see us make amends for mistakes we make, this is an indirect lesson on discipline and humility for them to learn. They learn a lot from your action and not just words. Parents should apologetically and remorsefully show repentance to their kids for wrong doings when necessary – this is true humility and it shows a humble heart. It is like being in the laboratory of life with your kids. You can teach them with a million words on humility, but there is nothing as strong as the practical side of humility displayed to children from their parents. 2 Timothy 2:2 declares: "And the things that thou hast heard of me among many witnesses, the same commit thou to faithful men, who shall be able to teach others also". This is how we can, through these moments, commit what we have heard, to the next generation of men and women that are currently in our "laboratory of life".

One major struggle that kids face today is the temptations of the internet in the form of too much time spent online, inappropriate things watched online, chatting with the wrong people, etc. Recently, my child was struggling with watching shows on "Youtube" that I had not authorized, when she was supposed to be doing her homework. After redirecting her to resist the temptation and she kept falling for the temptation to watch shows instead of using the computer for schoolwork, I decided to utilize "external blocking" – block the website she was accessing. After doing this, my eyes were opened to the principle of "internal resisting" and "external blocking". With regards to disciplining and training a child, it is important to implement and pay more attention to the principle of "internal resisting" versus "external blocking". Internal resisting is teaching a child to personally resist temptation from within, rather than you externally withdrawing or blocking the temptation from them. While external blocking is good and can be applicable in certain circumstances, if a child is trained to internally resist temptations and evil, he or she will have more internal strength to resist the devil (James 4:7) and even deal with peer pressure and bullying. One of the rules in our house that we established with our children is that they would guard their eyes and ears from any negative influence, for example bad television programs, ungodly music, etc. "Keep thy heart with all diligence; for out of it are the issues of life" (Proverbs 4:23). We taught them to "abstain from all appearance of evil" (1 Thessalonians 5:22). We saw a very refreshing result of instilling this principle when our child was just about 3 years old. We visited a family that we knew and perceived had similar or even more godly values with training kids. We were so comfortable with allowing our child to interact freely with theirs and we let her go play without our supervision. They were watching a television show and I just happened to go check on her wellbeing after a long of time. To my amazement, my child was sitting in the back of the room with her head turned facing the wall while others were watching the program. I came by her side and inquired what was wrong and she responded that they were watching a "bad show" that she could not watch. This is internal resisting – being able to personally resist the lure of temptation in preference for obedience, even despite the presence of peer pressure. You will not always be with your children, therefore, you must mold them to make sound decisions autonomously like Daniel. "But Daniel purposed in his heart that he would not defile himself with the portion of the king's meat, nor with the wine which he drank…" (Daniel 1:8). Internal resisting can be seen in the life of Joseph the dreamer (Genesis 39:7-12), and Jesus, the son of God (Matthew 4:1-11). God the Father did not block Jesus from facing temptation but allowed him to build strong resistance against sin. Internal resistance requires effort from both the parent (trainer) and child (trainee). Whilst external blocking is an easy and simpler step, internal resistance requires training (time and patience). It takes more effort to develop the internal resistance than to simply just remove or block the temptation. These days, parents are looking more and more for easy solutions to training kids and external blocking seems an easy way out. However, external blocking can be applicable or beneficial in certain circumstances, for example when (1) providing boundaries especially when the consequences can be fatal or detrimental (i.e. putting sharp objects or candles out of reach); (2) when you are starting to train them late when they are used to a wrong pattern. For example, you have a teenage child that always went out with your car to pursue evil while you were at work. Now you want to make things right by taking away the key (while teaching them the right way, so they don't feel the blocking means you don't love them anymore). Example 1 is the principle of external blocking in isolation, while example 2 is the principle of external blocking in conjunction with internal resisting.

Another vital aspect of discipline is financial discipline. When Jesus was on earth, he taught, performed miracles, preached and cast out devils (Luke 4:18). When he was discipling his selected twelve, he transitioned them from watching, to doing what he did (Matthew 10:8, Mark 16:15, John 14:12). They went from being passive observers to active participants in his ministry on earth. As parents, our goals should also be that our children are transitioned from "getting" to "earning". There are many adults today who do not fully understand the concept of financial responsibility or even work ethics because they were not discipled in this area. The main goal of this is not even about adding to the financial resource of the family (depending on family dynamics), it is more so about teaching the kids about responsibility, discipline and ingenuity. "Getting" to "earning" does not necessarily imply sending kids to work outside the home. Simply giving them affordable stipends in exchange for responsibilities they have at home could be helpful. Kids are excited to earn, and it teaches them how to handle money and diligence. Many who started out with this type of responsibility as kids, have turned out to be great entrepreneurs later in life. To further inspire the entrepreneurial spirit within them, encourage your children to develop ways to earn money, for example a lemonade stand.

Four: **Be engaged**. Truly, there is no substitute for engaged parents. Sure, today in our society, the television and the iPad have become the babysitters, and in many cases, the primary instructor. Children are being discipled by and learn how to live through actors who portray fantasies, and who may not reflect the morals we hold dear. One of the joys of parenthood is seeing your kids smile when you actively engage in their lives. Engaged parents must intentionally shun selfishness and avoid self-centered pursuits. Parents who are self-centered abandon their kids both physically and emotionally. Most people can easily see physical abandonment, but emotional abandonment can be an invisible problem.

As engaged parents, we must actively teach our children to submit to the Holy Spirit. This requires that we be submitted first. God has a prerequisite for His overflowing presence in our lives: we have to be thirsty!

What does thirst look like? Imagine having to trudge through the Sahara Desert on foot for 2 days after drinking a cup of saltwater, and in the blistering heat of the day, catching a glimpse of an oasis about a 3-minute walk away. What do you do at this moment? You would probably use every ounce of energy you have to fight your way to the life spring. That's thirst! Isaiah 44:3-4 declares: "For I will pour water upon him that is thirsty, and floods upon the dry grounds: I will pour my spirit upon thy seed, and my blessing upon thine offspring: and they shall spring up as among the grass, as willows by the water courses". God promises to prosper the way of our children when we as engaged parents teach them to seek Him with all of their heart.

"And the child grew, and waxed strong in spirit, and was in the desserts till the day of his showing unto Israel" Luke 1:80.

Non-Traditional Parents

There can be diverse types of non-traditional parents such as stepparents, as well as adoptive parents. In both situations, the parents are not blood parents but are still parents. As earlier stated, – **family is not necessarily your blood and blood is not always your family. Family is more significant or deeper than blood. Joseph's brothers were his blood, but they did not treat him as family, not even as a friend. Esau and Jacob were blood, but they did not always act as family. David and Jonathan were not blood, but they acted like brothers (family). Even Joseph, the father of Jesus was Jesus' father, but had no blood connection to Jesus. Your wife is the closest family to you, but she is not your blood. However, she is your flesh and your bone (Genesis 2:21-23). As a matter of fact, she is one with you and you are one with her (Genesis 2:24)!** In this regard, whether you are an adoptive parent, or a step parent, you are still a parent; and God has given you the opportunity and privilege to pour out his love in you upon another person in a very unique way – as a parent. There should be no room for negative sentiments, reservations or restrictions as we show God's love to them like as we would, if they were our own biological offspring. I know of stepparents and adoptive parents who love their step and adoptive kids in a way that an outsider cannot tell that there is no blood connection. The love of God cuts through our earthly sentiments and is without partiality and hypocrisy. "Charity suffereth long, and is kind; charity envieth not; charity vaunteth not itself, is not puffed up, Doth not behave itself unseemly, seeketh not her own, is not easily provoked, thinketh no evil" (1 Corinthians 13:4, 5). If we remember, we are also adopted into the family of God. "For ye have not received the spirit of bondage again to fear; but ye have received the Spirit of adoption, whereby we cry, Abba, Father" (Romans 8:15). "Having predestinated us unto the adoption of children by Jesus Christ to himself, according to the good pleasure of his will (Ephesians 1:5). James 1: 27 declares that: "religion that

God our Father accepts as pure and faultless is this: to look after orphans and widows in their distress and to keep oneself from being polluted by the world". Therefore, do not be skeptical about adoption if that is the step God is leading and directing you towards! "A father of the fatherless, a defender of widows, God sets the solitary in families; He brings out those who are bound into prosperity...." (Proverbs 68: 5, 6).

In addition to stepparents and adoptive parents, another angle to non-traditional parenting is single parenting. Hagar and the widow of Zarephath are examples of singles parents in the Bible.

Hagar was the mother of Ishmael, the son of Abraham. She became a single mother when she was forced out of the camp of Abraham to wander aimlessly in the dessert. She and Ishmael were in a hopeless situation and on the verge of death. Frustration and despair brought her to her knees (Genesis 21:16). She had given up, and in agony, abandoned her son (Genesis 21:15, 16). Ishmael, though all alone, knew to call on God. At the sound of Ishmael's voice God sympathetically reached out to deliver them. God answered their cries and became the provider and protector that they needed (Genesis 21:17-20). Therefore, as a single parent (whether man or woman), know that God hears the cries of your heart and is moved with compassion for your little ones (Genesis 21:17). Though the situation seems bleak, don't give up, persevere, God hears your cries and He will surely make a way for you!

The widow of Zarephath (1 Kings 17) was also a single parent. The family was experiencing a dire financial situation so severe that the widow had resolved that she and her son would just eat their last meal and die (1 Kings 17:12). But God had a different plan! Whilst a single parent might be concerned about how they will survive till the next day, God's plan could be using that same single parent to feed a nation! God used the widow to come to the aid of his prophet by providing him food to eat. Her unselfish act of submission (in accordance to God's will) to the prophet by giving her last, opened the door of great abundance for her family. God promised her: "...The barrel of meal shall not waste, neither shall the cruse of oil fail, until the day that the LORD sendeth rain upon the earth" (1 Kings 17:16). The message to gain from the story of the widow is similar to that of Hagar. God sees and understands the unique challenges that come with bringing up children without a spouse. He promises to stand firm and support you by providing for your every need. He will be the father or mother to your children that will help them grow in His grace.

CHAPTER 3

(BECOMING THE CHILD GOD INTENDED FOR MY PARENTS)

"Children, obey your parents in the Lord:
for this is right" (Ephesians 6:1)

Becoming a Godly Child

To be a godly child, it is important to be obedient to God and your parents (Ephesians 6:1, Colossians 3:20). When we are obedient to God, God can use us to be a part of history, by using us to be a part of his miraculous acts (John 6:1-14). It is important to note that being a son of a preacher does not mean that we know the Lord. Eli was a priest but his sons did not know God. "Now the sons of Eli were sons of Belial; they knew not the LORD" (1 Samuel 2:12). However, Samuel was dedicated and devoted to God (1 Samuel 2:18), and he learned how to hear the voice of God as a child (1 Samuel 3:10). Children can learn to hear God's voice and commune with God. Hearing the voice of God is not based on age or years of being in church, it is based on tuning your ears and heart to God by being dedicated and devoted to God.

"Children, obey your parents in the Lord: for this is right. Honour thy father and mother; which is the first commandment with promise; That it may be well with thee, and thou mayest live long on the earth (Ephesians 6:1-3).

"Children, obey your parents in all things: for this is well pleasing unto the Lord" (Colossians 3:20).

"But Samuel ministered before the Lord, being a child, girded with a linen ephod" (1 Samuel 2:18).

"And the Lord came, and stood, and called as at other times, Samuel, Samuel. Then Samuel answered, Speak; for thy servant heareth" (1 Samuel 3:10).

CHAPTER 4

(BECOMING THE GRANDPARENT GOD INTENDED FOR MY GRANDKIDS)

"Children's children are the crown of old men; and the glory of children are their father's" Proverbs 17:6

The Beauty of Grandkids

After you have "sown" for many years (sometimes in tears) into your children, and have laid the foundation for them to be servants of our Father, soon the time comes that you have the opportunity to "reap" the joy of the first grandchild (Psalms 126:5). What a delight to see your generations! To behold the glory of God expanding your family and continuing your legacy. An unexplainable sense of accomplishment, like icing on the cake. The Bible calls this moment a "crown" (Proverbs 17:6). In other words, you are being honored for your leadership and sacrifice. Grandchildren are the culmination of hard work and relentless dedication to the development of children after God's heart. They are the reward for your labor and a "slap" in the face of the enemy who wants your expectation to be cut off, and your seed destroyed (John 10:10). Be confident that the first and all grandchildren to come in succession WILL follow the legacy of Christ as savior that you laid down for your heritage. The word declares in Proverbs 22:6 that we should "Train up a child in the way he should go: and when he is old, he will not depart from it".

At this stage, the beauty of the scriptures: "yea, thou shalt see thy children's children, and peace upon Israel"(Psalms 128:6); and "thy wife shall be as a fruitful vine by the sides of thine house: thy children like olive plants round about thy table" (Psalms 128:3) becomes a joy. Grandparents have a very significant role in their grandchildren's lives. As "watchmen", (those who stand guard to protect others) grandparents should surround their grandchildren securely in prayer. Daily, they must intercede on their behalf combating the plans of the enemy to choke them with the cares of the world (Matthew 13:22). As "curators" of family heritage and tradition, grandparents must take time to tell the stories of family history and establish and carry on traditions that bond relationships. When young ones learn about the family legacy, those who paved the way before them, and the challenges and triumphs they experienced, it helps to shape their identity, and helps them feel more secure in who they are. As "counselors", grandparents must be a sympathetic listening ear, and an imparter of sound advice. Grandchildren will greatly benefit from the wisdom you share from your life lessons and experiences.

"A good man leaveth an inheritance to his children's children..." Proverbs 13:22

An Inheritance for Children's Children (Grandchildren)

More than houses, cars, money, and land, the greatest inheritance a grandparent can leave their grandchild is a blessing through the legacy of Christ. In Genesis 48, Jacob blessed his grandchildren. He spoke life over them and framed their future with his words. As grandparents, you have a duty to command a blessing over your grandchildren in accordance to God's word. God made us in His image, therefore we have the power to create with our words as He did from the very beginning. The creative power within our words will be a catalyst for victory in their lives.

It is also very important as parents and grandparents that we plan the earthly wellbeing of our children and grandchildren by means of financial discipline and financial planning. If we just live our lives for the moment, and enjoy vacations, gadgets, cars, name brand clothes in our prime time, without any foresight to provide and advantage to our future generations, then we are not living according to God's plan for us as a present or future grandparent. Therefore, wills are important; life insurance is beneficial; wise investments can be helpful; family connections and networks are instrumental; buying houses so your generations don't have to rent is strategic; leaving a business or businesses down the family line so your generations don't have to submit resumes is an advantage; and encouraging entrepreneurship is vital. All of these examples are some ways we can leave a physical inheritance for our generations. You might not be able to do all of these but if you can do all, do all; if you can do only one or a few, do what is within your reach and ability! If you cannot even do any, leave a spiritual blessing and legacy for your generations!

CHAPTER 5

(BECOMING THE INLAW GOD INTENDED FOR MY INLAWS)

"And Ruth said, Intreat me not to leave thee, or to return from following after thee: for whither thou goest, I will go; and where thou lodgest, I will lodge: thy people shall be my people, and thy God my God" Ruth 1:16

"Your people Shall be My People…"

Ruth and Naomi are an ideal example of an in-law relationship in the Bible. Both had character traits that all married people can emulate when relating with in-laws. First, Naomi was the ideal mother in law. She was kind, compassionate and loving (Ephesians 4:32). She blessed her daughters-in-law (Ruth 1:8-9). She took them as her own, calling them her daughters (Ruth1:12). When she announced that she was leaving, they didn't want to leave her and even wept at the thought (Ruth 1:9). Their reaction affirms that she was good to them. Furthermore, her actions after Ruth chose to stay by her side demonstrates her love. Naomi officially had no more ties to Ruth when her son (Ruth's husband) died, yet she chose to take her under her wing and care for her and teach her how to thrive. Naomi looked out for Ruth's wellbeing and had the wisdom to help secure her future (Ruth 3:1). To accomplish this, Naomi trained Ruth on how to get a husband (Ruth 3:3-4). The end result of Naomi's love and dedication was her own restoration (Ruth 4:15).

Equally, Ruth was an exemplary daughter-in-law. She was committed and loyal. Ruth desired so much to be a part of Naomi to blend as one. Even when her husband died, and Ruth could have chosen to return to her old family, she chose to stay by her mother-in-law's side (Ruth 1:16-17). She left all she knew behind to embrace her new family and even a new land. She did not try to hold on tightly to her former life. Sometimes when people get married, they allow their previous family to have too much influence over their new family. This makes the process of "leaving and cleaving" more challenging. When a person is committed to opening their heart and expanding their capacity to love their new family, they have a better opportunity to develop a good bond with their in-laws. Remember, family is not just about blood connections. God is the one who divinely orchestrates family in various ways.

Along with being loyal, Ruth was teachable. After arriving in their new homeland, Naomi had to teach Ruth their ways of life. She also had to teach her how to show Boaz that she desired to be his wife. What Naomi instructed her to do was no doubt risky and probably downright nerve-wrecking and embarrassing. But Ruth wholeheartedly followed her instructions (Ruth 3:5). She didn't react in pride with a know-it-all attitude. She trusted Naomi and submitted to wisdom. Likewise, when interacting with in-laws, when given sound advice, don't reject it because you know everything, and you don't want to be told what to do. With God's help, receive the correction or piece of advice humbly. It will positively impact your relationship. Finally, Ruth was willing to serve. She was not just interested in what she could get, but she gave of herself unselfishly. She worked on Naomi's behalf, gleaning from Boaz's fields (Ruth 2:2). Her hard work spoke for her and even Boaz had to take notice (Ruth 2:11-12). In the end she was rewarded for her desire to serve Naomi, and she was remembered throughout history. Each one of us can leave a legacy and make significant impact on our families by simply having a servant's heart.

Therefore, whether you are a father-in-law, mother-in-law, son-in-law, daughter-in-law, brother-in-law, sister-in-law, "friend-in-law", or any other type of in-law relationship you are in, always ensure you play a loving and constructive role just as seen in the example of Ruth and Naomi. With this, there will be lasting peace and joy for everyone!

"Who rejoice to do evil..." Proverbs 2:14

Dealing with "Pharaohic" In-Laws

Whereas, Naomi was so nice and loving to her daughter-in-law Ruth, such that she always wanted to remain with Naomi, there are in-laws who are so mean, wicked, selfish, bossy and even heartless, that people do not want to be around them. I term these people as "Pharaohic in-laws". Remember in the scriptures, Pharaoh was so evil, that the Israelites wanted to leave speedily (Exodus 3:7). But pharaoh denied them exit from Egypt until the mighty deliverer (Isaiah 49:24), the God of Abraham rescued them, disgracing all the chariots of Pharaoh and killing the firstborn sons of Egypt. Therefore, if you are dealing with any Pharaohic in-law, the God of Abraham will set you free!

In the story of Jacob and Laban, Laban can be considered a "Pharaohic" in-law. Whilst Naomi was a "pull" factor to her in-laws (Ruth and Orpah) (Ruth 1:10), Laban was a "push" factor to his in-law Jacob. A "pull" factor can be described as an attraction while a "push" factor can be described as a repellant. At a point in their relationship, Laban was selfish, self-seeking, deceptive and cruel to his son-in-law (Genesis 29 & 30) which made Jacob his son-in-law wants to flee from him (Genesis 31:20).To avoid repelling our in-laws like Laban, it is important to always check our motives when interacting, and seek to show love.

"For, brethren, ye have been called unto liberty;
only use not liberty for an occasion to the flesh,
but by love serve one another" Galatians 5:13

In-law Attitudes

After evaluating the different examples of in-law relationships displayed in the bible, we can see that there are several different attitudes that in-laws portray:

1. Naomi – A very pleasant and desirable in-law to have
2. Laban – A "Pharaohic" in-law who can repel people
3. Ruth – A teachable, humble and embracing in-law who embraced her new family whole-heartedly
4. Jacob – A run away in-law who runs from unpleasant in-laws or experiences (Genesis 31:20)
5. Orpah – A neutral in-law who is not fighting anyone, but chooses to face their own destiny and future separately (Ruth 1:14, 15) – a "neutral" factor. Even Abraham, <u>directed by the wisdom of God</u>, had this approach with his nephew, Lot (Genesis 13:9). The bible admonishes us to live peaceably with all men (Romans 12:18). That is why Abraham chose to live separately from Lot to avoid strife (Genesis 13:7). Sometimes, the wiser choice is to not be around or close to our extended relations. "And the land was not able to bear them, that they might dwell together: for their substance was great, so that they could not dwell together". Even though there is separation, peace and love can remain. After Abraham and Lot parted, Abraham, still full of the love of God for Lot his nephew, went to fight for him when Lot was in a battle (Genesis 14). Furthermore, when God wanted to destroy Lot's habitation, Abraham, still full of God's love for Lot (even though separated), prayed and interceded for Lot's deliverance and God's mercy on Lot's family (Genesis 18).

Examine your life as an in-law. Are you a "pull" or a "push" ("Pharaohic") factor to the in-laws that God has brought your way? Are you like Naomi, who in-laws want to embrace and remain with, or are you like Laban, who Jacob (the son-in-law) wanted to flee far from (Genesis 31:20)? If you cannot be a "pull" factor like Naomi, don't be a "push" factor like Laban; rather be a "neutral" factor like Orpah.

CHAPTER 6

(GOD PUTS THE SOLUTUDE IN FAMILY)

"He hath made everything beautiful in His time"! Ecclesiastes 3:11

Single and Eligible?

After being the blessing God intended you to be to your parents as a child growing within the frame of your parents' household, the time comes for you to create a family of your own. "To everything there is a season, and a time to every purpose under the heaven" (Ecclesiastes 3:1). At this point in life, it is important that the single person is constantly preparing for marriage even before the potential life partner is discovered. One of the most essential ways you can prepare for the arrival of your spouse is by praying for your spouse years before you know them (and afterwards). Furthermore, you can prepare for your marriage by praying for your children way ahead of their birth (and afterwards). The prayers you pray now, will give you an advantage in the future! If you ask the Holy Spirit, He will give you the words to pray. When I was a teenager I started praying for my spouse. I would pray for specific things that God would share with me about their life, and I hadn't even met them yet! Through spending time in prayer, God also shared glimpses of my spouse with me in dreams, and I was reassured of the kind of person they would be. I encourage you, in your pursuit for a spouse (Proverbs 31:10; Proverbs 20:6), pursue God and He will guide you and give you the desires of your heart.

What makes one ready for marriage? People spend a huge amount of time, money, effort, and much more preparing for their wedding and ignore vital preparation for their marriage. They forget that the wedding is only one day (even a few hours, or a few minutes for some), whilst the marriage is a lifetime. The following areas of preparations must therefore be developed thoroughly as one prepares for marriage:

- Spiritual Preparation
- Emotional Preparation
- Financial Preparation

You are single, but how do you know you are eligible? Are you spiritually ready? Are you financially steady? Are you emotionally mature? Are you equipped for the inevitable challenges ahead? This is because marriage is not a bed of roses as many people think or assume. The challenges of marriage are far beyond the stories we read about and see in movies. They can be too difficult to deal with if we are not adequately prepared. Therefore, use your time wisely in singleness. God surely makes all things beautiful in His time. He will beautify your life with a blessed marriage in due season. Even if: you feel like you are too old ("crossed over" the age of marriage); you are "neglected" (ignored and abandoned by God and man); or you are not married when you think you should be married because of other circumstances; there is still hope in God! God will make a way where there seems to be no way (Isaiah 41:18).

"But the Lord said unto Samuel, Look not on his countenance, or on the height of his stature; because I have refused him: for the Lord seeth not as man seeth; for man looketh on the outward appearance, but the Lord looketh on the heart" 1 Samuel 16:7

Biblical Wisdom for Choosing a Life Partner

Choosing a life partner is one of the most important decisions in one's life. As such, the best way to do this is by tapping into the wisdom of God and seeking divine direction in the process. Genesis 24 is a theological masterpiece of the various steps and stages in choosing one's spouse. Below is a verse by verse dissection of the hidden wisdom found in Genesis 24.

*Genesis 24:1 & 2 – "And Abraham was **old**, and **well stricken in age**…"; and Genesis 24:2 – "And Abraham said unto his **eldest** servant…" – these speak of right timing and maturity. Marriage is not for kids or those who are immature.

*Genesis 24:1 – "and the Lord had **blessed** Abraham in all things" – many people think of blessing as just material stuff, but the blessing of God is not limited to material things. For example, Psalm 119: 1 declares "blessed are the undefiled in the way, who walk in the law of the Lord". You need to take the blessing of God to your marriage so the other person can partake in the blessing of God which is not limited to money. As a matter of fact, a person can be blessed but not have wealth. Blessing is spiritual. The consequence of blessing will show up in prosperity. Proverbs 10:22 declares: "The blessing of the Lord, it maketh rich, and he addeth no sorrow with it". The timing of the prosperity that comes from being blessed is in God's hands (Ecclesiastes 3:11). Many have financial wealth but lack the blessing of God. Seek the blessing of the Lord, not money.

*Genesis 24:4 – "**but thou shalt go** unto my country, and to my **kindred**, and take a wife unto my son Isaac" – the search for a spouse is a mission or an assignment. It must be taken seriously. Also, a spouse should be from the family of God – someone who really knows the Lord (2 Corinthians 6:14).

*Genesis 24:11, 12, 13, 14 – "And he made his camels to kneel down without the city by a well of water at the time of the evening, **even the time that women go out to draw water**" – this is the seeking part that men need to do; Genesis 24:12 – "**And he said, O Lord God of my master Abraham, I pray thee,** send me good speed this day, and shew kindness unto my master Abraham" – you will need to ask God for guidance and direction in this process; Genesis 24:13 & 14 – "Behold, I stand here by the well of water; and the daughters of the men of the city come out to draw water: and let it come to pass, that the damsel **to whom I shall say,** Let down thy pitcher, I pray thee, that I may drink; and she shall say, Drink, and I will give thy camels drink also: let the same be she that thou hast appointed for thy servant Isaac; and thereby shall I know that thou hast shewed kindness unto my master" – this is the "knocking" part for men. Not only do men need to seek, ask God for guidance, but they also have to "knock" by reaching out to who they perceive is God's plan for their life.

*Genesis 24:15 – "And it came to pass, **before he had done speaking, that, behold, Rebekah came out**…" – Summarily for men, choosing a life partner can be as easy as Matthew 7:7 & 8 which says "Ask, and it shall be given you; seek, and ye shall find; knock, and it shall be opened unto you: for every one that asketh receiveth; and he that seeketh findeth; and to him that knocketh it shall be opened".

*Genesis 24:16 – "And the damsel was very **fair** to look upon, a **virgin, neither had any man known her: and she went down to the well, and filled her pitcher, and came up**" – this verse speaks to the woman's preparations for marriage. Keep yourselves looking good or attractive and keep yourselves undefiled. In keeping yourselves looking good and undefiled, let 1 Peter 3:3 be your guide: "Whose adorning let it not be that outward adorning of plaiting the hair, and of wearing of gold, or of putting on of apparel; but let it be the hidden man of the heart, in that which is not corruptible, even the ornament of a meek and quiet spirit, which is in the sight of God of great price". It must be pointed out that being attractive can be as simple as taking a shower and brushing your teeth! Being attractive does not necessarily mean heavy makeup, dyed hair, plastic surgery, etc. God has made everyone beautiful already and you can celebrate your beauty even in very simple ways. Psalm 139:14: "I will praise thee; for I am fearfully and wonderfully made: marvellous are thy works; and that my soul knoweth right well". In addition to keeping yourself attractive and undefiled, a woman should make herself able to be found by going where you are supposed to go and doing what you are supposed to do. In other words, be occupied with your day to day business and don't sit at home all day every day!

*Genesis 24:17, 18 – **"And the servant ran to meet her, and said, Let me, I pray thee, drink a little water of thy pitcher. And she said, Drink, my lord: and she hasted, and let down her pitcher upon her hand, and gave him drink."** – When you make yourself as a woman "seek-able", your God-sent man will approach you speedily. Always have a friendly disposition as you never know what man you are speaking to; he might be the answer to your prayers that you've been waiting for! Hebrews 13:2 – "Be not forgetful to entertain strangers: for thereby some have entertained angels unawares". While having a friendly disposition, be wise because we live in a very sinful and wicked world. Matthew 10:16 – "Behold, I send you forth as sheep in the midst of wolves: be ye therefore wise as serpents, and harmless as doves". Galatians 6:10 – "As we have therefore opportunity, let us do good unto all men, especially unto them who are of the household of faith". Practicing a friendly disposition before marriage can be a good way to practice living peacefully when married (Hebrews 12:24)! Also, be humble and submissive; and not prideful even if you have all the money that you think he does not have. Rebecca had more in the moment (water) while the man was so thirsty and lacked (water) at the moment, but she was still humble and called him "my lord". Eventually Rebecca's humility paid off when she married the son of Abraham whom God has so blessed in all things (Genesis 24:1).

*Genesis 24:19, 20 – "And when she had done giving him drink, she said, **I will draw water for thy camels also, until they have done drinking. And she hasted, and emptied her pitcher into the trough, and ran again unto the well to draw water, and drew for all his camels"** – go the extra mile in being kindhearted. Hebrews 13:16 – "But to do good and to communicate forget not: for with such sacrifices God is well pleased". Show signs of servanthood, humility and submission for God resists the proud but gives grace to the humble (1 Peter 5:5).

*Genesis 24:21 – **"And the man wondering at her held his peace, to wit whether the Lord had made his journey prosperous or not"** – when you follow's God's directions as a woman, you make it easier for the man to confirm in his heart, the leading of God. At this stage, a man must pay close observation and not rush.

*Genesis 24:22 – **"And it came to pass, as the camels had done drinking, that the man took a golden earring of half a shekel weight,**

and two bracelets for her hands of ten shekels weight of gold" – in this verse, the man shows interest and gets her some gifts. Gifts are simple ways a man can communicate his interest in a lady.

*Genesis 24:23 – "and said, **Whose daughter art thou? tell me, I pray thee: is there room in thy father's house for us to lodge in?**" – after interest is developed and shown, a man must inquire about the woman and her family.

*Genesis 24:24, 25 – Rebecca confirms her identity as within the kindred circle that was required. This means we must ensure that the person is truly a child of God. Friendship was thereafter built and she welcomed him to meet her family.

*Genesis 24:26, 27 – At this point, the man had confirmation in his heart that Rebecca was the perfect will of God. At this point, he worshipped the Lord!

*Genesis 24:28-32 – Family introduction, family acceptance and family hospitality takes place.

*Genesis 24:33 – "And there was set meat before him to eat: **but he said, I will not eat, until I have told mine errand**" – the man was focused on his assignment (marriage) and avoided any distraction. Sometimes, even after finding the right one, men can lose their focus and be distracted before the marriage. It is important to stay focused. "Flee fornication… (1 Corinthians 6:18), intimacy will come later; be focused on your future family and avoid other female distractions.

*Genesis 24:34-49 – be clear to her family about your intentions with sincerity. Although Rebecca had already told them (Genesis 24:28), he still spoke himself.

*Genesis 24:50, 51 – it is good to get confirmation and permission from the lady's family upon speaking your intentions. That way, the lady is released to go be with her husband (Genesis 2:24).

*Genesis 24:52 – he bowed to God in worship after consent from the lady's family (2nd confirmation – one from God in verse 26 and verse 27, then from the lady's family). Heavenly and earthly confirmations because out of the mouth or two or more witnesses, every word is established (Deuteronomy 17:6, Deuteronomy 19:15, Matthew 18:16, 2 Corinthians 13:1). Many say they heard from God with no other witness and it might just even be their flesh or senses not God! In marriage, it is good to hear from God and get a confirmation from God through whatever or whomever or however he chooses to confirm!

*Genesis 24:53 – gifts are given to the lady and her family as a show of love, honor and respect.

*Genesis 24:54 – **"And they did eat and drink, he and the men that were with him,** and tarried all night; and they rose up in the morning, and he said, Send me away unto my master" – mission accomplished so they can celebrate now. Celebration here is symbolic of the wedding.

*Genesis 24:55-58 – protect her after she is given to become yours, let no one take her away seeing the Lord hath given her to you. She also must be willing to protect the union and let everyone know that she is yours.

*Genesis 24:59, 60 – parental blessing is good as she goes with you.

*Genesis 24:61 – **"And Rebekah arose, and her damsels, and they rode upon the camels, and followed the man**: and the servant took Rebekah, and went his way" – from this point on, the lady follows the man. Ruth 1:16, 17 – "…Intreat me not to leave thee, or to return from following after thee: for whither thou goest, I will go; and where thou lodgest, I will lodge: thy people shall be my people, and thy God my God: where thou diest, will I die, and there will I be buried: the Lord do so to me, and more also, if ought but death part thee and me". Genesis 2:24 – "Therefore shall a man leave his father and his mother, and shall cleave unto his wife: and they shall be one flesh".

*Genesis 24:62-66 – the joy and reality of marriage dawns.

*Genesis 24:67 – **"And Isaac brought her into his mother Sarah's tent, and took Rebekah, and she became his wife; and he loved her**: and Isaac was comforted after his mother's death" – the blessed home begins. Genesis 2:25 – "And they were both naked, the man and his wife, and were not ashamed".

"For the lips of a strange woman drop as an honeycomb, and her mouth is smoother than oil: But her end is bitter as wormwood, sharp as a two-edged sword" Proverbs 5:3, 4

Lessons for Singles from Samson's Life

One of the most famous couples in the Bible is Samson and Delilah. Interestingly enough, this was probably one of the most prominent examples of what singles should NOT do when wanting to get married. There are several lessons we can learn from the actions and consequences that unfold in Samson's life:

One: **Choose a mate in God.** This statement itself can be interpreted in two ways: First, you should choose a mate through the leading of the Holy Spirit (in God). In Judges 14, Samson first encounters a Philistine woman thathe determines he wants to marry, just based on a mere look. There is no mention of Samson asking God to show him his wife, or of him spending time observing her behavior, or even asking the advice of others more experienced. It simply starts off by saying "And Samson went down to Timnah, and saw a woman in Timnah of the daughters of the Philistines" (Judges 14:1). It's interesting that it says he went "***down* to Timnah**"! Sometimes as singles, will reduce our standards and settle for less by going *down* to "Timnah" (clubs, wild parties, bars, sexualized online chat forums, worldly concerts, etc.), just to alleviate our loneliness. The results of diminished standards can be detrimental to your destiny. In contrast, in Genesis chapter 24, when the servant of Abraham searches for a spouse for Isaac, he first consults God and he spends time observing her actions and character. This requires that you earnestly seek and practice hearing and submitting to His voice. Spending time in quietness and meditation can help you practice discerning the voice of God. Knowing the voice of God can truly bring the peace you need to make right decisions, and bring calm in any stormy situation. One good example was Jesus in the Garden of Gethsemane (Matthew 26:36-44). He went there in the night to pray during a time of great distress. He also separated himself and prayed alone. Why? He knew that he had to get away from the distractions of companions – those who might try to talk Him out of doing things God's way. He knew He had to hear God's voice of assurance when He had to make an immensely tough decision to surrender His life. **You never want to make life altering decisions without the peace of God**! If you seek Him, the Father will give you the assurance you need to pursue or abort or your plans.

Second, you should choose a mate who themselves are in God (a person after God's heart – 1 Samuel 13:14). Samson was a man that was given the distinction to be set apart and chosen by God from birth, yet he reduced his worth and chose to lie with prostitutes. He forsook the call of God to follow his fleshly desires and chose to keep the company of those who did not follow the will of God. Samson suffered dire consequences as a result of his foolish choices in relationships. In 1 Corinthians 15:33, it says "Be not deceived: evil communications corrupt good manners". Therefore, if you involve yourself with someone who is not in God, you will ultimately change for the worst. It is therefore essential to submit our every relationship or relationship prospect to the Lord. A good example of this is seen through the way God orchestrated the first marriage. In Genesis 2:21, it says that after Adam had searched through all the animals and could not find one who complemented him, he stood in the presence of God. God, knowing it was time for Adam to meet his wife, caused a deep sleep to come upon him. This signifies two things. First, Adam had to surrender and completely trust God in the process of obtaining his wife. **God made him sleep to show us to rest and not stress over this issue of finding someone**. When you rest in him (Matthew 11:28), is when you will find the exact one God has for you! It is a wonderful feeling to totally rest in the peace of God, knowing He is capable, and you can trust Him. Second, **Adam's eyes were closed; therefore, he did not choose a wife by his own sight** (2 Corinthians 5:7), but he allowed the Lord to work on him from the inside out, to prepare him to receive the woman he fashioned to fit him perfectly. Adam said "this is now bone of my bone and flesh of my flesh..." (Genesis

2:23). In other words, I know she is the one because she has a piece of me inside of her and our Father put it there. Only the one God has for you can provide the strength and support you need (like a bone). *It is also interesting to note that the ribs are situated near the heart as protection. The wife God has for you will know you and your heart like no other human being on earth; and out of her love and devotion, she will protect it through praying for you, and being a listening ear. Proverbs 31:11 says your heart will safely trust in her.*

Two: **Don't be Led by Emotions.** Being led by emotions can cause you to lose your vision and even your life. Samson gave in to the nagging of Delilah and compromised his values, his commitment, and his integrity. He was drawn by his loneliness and her beauty, and ultimately it was his emotions that led to his horrific demise – losing both eyes at the hands of his enemies the Philistines. His eyes led him to Delilah and his eyes were sacrificed as the price of his being led by emotions. Likewise also when we let our emotions mislead us sexually, the reproductive organs that were created by God to procreate life can lead to death (through diseases) as opposed to creating life as God intended. His emotions led to his disobedience which led to his vision being taken and him being placed in a prison, chained and confined to a place where he grinded rock all day (Judges 16:21). He was now stuck in a monotonous demeaning cycle of going nowhere. He eventually died prematurely.

Three: **Seek and Receive Wise Counsel.** When it came to selecting a wife, Samson rejected the advice of his godly parents (Judges 14:3). Though they advised him to not seek a wife amongst the uncircumcised Philistines, Samson refused to obey. Like Samson many Christians have chosen to stray from their foundations and reject the wise words of godly parents, pastors or godly friends when selecting a mate. They often do this to silence any voice that will not validate their decision to be with someone who is unequally yoked (2 Corinthians 6:14). Though ignorance may be bliss for a time, when reality hits that you have made a huge mistake by ignoring sound judgement, your bliss quickly turns into misery. The bible says the following in Proverbs 11:14: "Where no counsel is, the people fall: but in the multitude of counsellors there is safety". As a wise man or woman of God, it is essential to lay aside pride and seek the advice from those who are seasoned, those whom you know will impart the wisdom of God into your life.

Four: **Stay Pure** (1 Corinthians 6:13-20). I know in our society today, purity has become a not-so-popular message, even in the church. Sex before marriage has seemingly become the norm. Self-professing Christians have settled for common-law unions, where unmarried people live together because of loneliness and financial convenience. Even, some people and cultures like to test the "baby factory" for "productivity". But God's standards NEVER change. God's word warns us to "flee fornication" (1 Corinthians 6:18, 1 Corinthians 10:8). In 1 Corinthians 7:2, it states: "Nevertheless, to avoid fornication, let every man have his own wife, and let every woman have her own husband". Samson did not abide by this instruction. Instead, he found himself continuously in the beds of strange women – women who were not his wife (Judges 16:1, 4). Not staying pure caused Samson to lose his covering – his hair (Judges 16:19). In other words, when you act outside of the will of God, you are no longer safely covered in his protection (Psalms 91:1). The bible reassures us of this fact in 2 Corinthians 6:14, when it states: "Be ye not unequally yoked together with unbelievers: for what *fellowship* hath righteousness with unrighteousness? and what communion hath *light* with *darkness*"? Choosing to engage in sex before marriage will break your communion with God because, He who is light, will not fellowship with darkness. The pleasures of the moment can ultimately come at a great cost.

Five: **Heed the Warning Signs.** When we think we have found a potential mate, we initially have that feeling of excitement. Every time that person calls our heart skips a beat or we get butterflies in our stomach. Generally, we begin to fall in love with the idea of being "in love". While having these feelings are natural, allowing them to blind you and cloud your judgement can be detrimental. This is evident in Samson's story. Samson had finally found someone to love in the person of Delilah. Delilah was beautiful and enticing. She knew how to manipulate Samson to get what she wanted and, unbeknownst to Samson, she also knew how to plan his downfall (Judges 16:19-20). It seems very unusual that after all the times Delilah tricked him, Samson still stayed by Delilah's side. His desire to be with her caused him to act as if he was completely oblivious to her schemes. Like Samson, our emotions and desires can distort our perception of reality. If the one you see as a potential mate is acting in an untrustworthy manner, if they are displaying a short temper, if they are acting contrary to their profession as a Christian, if you cannot see the fruit of the spirit, or if they are asking you to engage in pre-marital sex, then **heed the warning signs.** Though you may experience a *moment* of disappointment (perhaps because of the time you invested), you will potentially save yourself from a *lifetime* of heartache or even save your life from death.

The conclusion from the life of Samson can be seen in this scripture: **"How should one chase a thousand, and two put ten thousand to flight, except their Rock had sold them, and the LORD had shut them up?" (Deuteronomy 32:30). When Samson was single, God used him to chase a thousand. "And he found a new jawbone of an ass, and put forth his hand, and took it, and slew a thousand men therewith" (Judges 15:15). However, when Samson joined with Delilah, instead of slaying ten thousand as the scriptures says of two chasing ten thousand, <u>Samson was slain</u> (Judges 16:30). It is therefore extremely vital that you be led by God and not your mind or flesh when choosing a spouse.**

*"A father of the fatherless, and a
judge of the widows, is God in his
holy habitation" Psalms 68:5*

Widows and Widowers

God has a special place in his heart for those who have lost their spouse, and children who have lost their parents (Psalms 146:9). It is his desire that after the loss of a loved one, life can continue, and you can thrive. This includes finding another spouse (1 Corinthians 7: 8, 9) like Ruth did (Ruth 4:13). When choosing to remarry after being a widow or a widower, in addition to the guidelines mentioned previously to singles in general, there are unique considerations. For example, when choosing a mate, if you have children (especially younger children) you must cautiously observe how they interact with them. The person you are marrying must be willing to accept your children as their own. It will not be an easy process to blend the family, but with God, all things are possible. The blending of a new family will require wisdom, patience and the love of God from all parties involved.

Chapter 7

(DIVORCE)

"Let thy fountain be blessed: and rejoice with the wife of thy youth" Proverbs 5:18

Safeguarding your Marriage from Divorce

To safeguard your marriage from divorce, one nature or attribute of God is very critical for us to showcase and display. It is the attribute or nature of God that says God was, is and is to come (Revelation 1:8). In your marriage, your spouse should not just remember you as "was" nice, or "was" patient, etc.; but as "was" kind (patient, etc.), "is" kind (patient, etc.), and will always be kind (patient, etc.)! Let your good attributes not be a thing of the past in the sight of your spouse. Like as God does not change (Malachi 3:6), do not change or trade your good attributes for worse. Afterall, we are made in the image and likeness of God (Genesis 1:26)!

Wife, to keep your husband, you need to submit to your husband. **Submission makes it easier for your husband to love you**. It must be pointed out that men can be hard to live with. A former co-worker once pointed out that: **"men are hard to live with and hard to live without"**! Yet the scriptures says: "Wives, submit yourselves unto your own husbands, **as it is fit in the Lord**" (Colossians 3:18). Ephesians 5: says: "**Wives, submit** yourselves unto your own husbands, as unto the Lord. For the husband is the head of the wife, even as Christ is the head of the church: and he is the saviour of the body. Therefore as the church is subject unto Christ, so let the wives be to their own husbands **in every thing**". Notice that Ephesians 5 says wives should submit in everything while Colossians says wives should submit as it is fit in the Lord. There is no contradiction here. However, the two verses are complimentary, which means put together – wives submit to your husbands in everything as it is fit in the Lord. Therefore, if your husband asks you to kill someone, going only by Ephesians 5 (submit in everything), a wife may foolishly and ignorantly miss the voice of God. Submission to our husbands should be in everything as it is fit in the Lord. Submission to our husbands in everything as it is fit in the Lord has helped many godly women to endure long term pain (and abuse), and save their marriage from wreckage even when dealing with unsaved husbands. Notable examples of this are testimonies heard and read about Smith Wigglesworth's wife and Mrs. Deborah Powe (wife of late Pastor Greg Powe – Revealing Truth Ministries in Tampa Florida). In order to perfect submission, a wife must grow and mature significantly in her **attitude**. Someone recently pointed out in a speech about the importance of the woman's attitude in a relationship:

"a lady can be attractive, but the man still leaves;
a lady can be beautiful, but still dumped;
a lady can be a great cook, and still abandoned;
a lady can have a gorgeous figure, yet abandoned;
a lady can bring great pleasure, but still dumped;
a lady can be rich and so wealthy, but still abandoned;
a lady can be so made up every day, but still later rejected;
if a lady has a bad attitude, it does not guarantee keeping a man;
only a good attitude can keep a man".

The summary of having a good attitude as a woman in your marriage is that – **getting a man is easy and anyone can get a man (even a prostitute); however, only your submission (through your attitude) can keep a man.** That's why the resounding admonishment for wives in the bible is to submit to their own husbands!

Husband, to keep your wife, you need to love to your wife. "Husbands, love your wives, and be not bitter against them" (Colossians 3:19). **You**

cannot love what you disregard. "If ye love me, keep my commandments" (John 14:15). When you love your wife, you will affirm her (assure her of her value and worth) and reassure her of your love for her through words and actions. Furthermore, to love your wife means to:

One: Be committed (spirit, soul and body). Being committed means that she is your only treasure and that you flee adultery. "Marriage is honourable in all, and the bed undefiled: but whoremongers and adulterers God will judge" (Hebrews 13:4). Being committed also means that she is your only treasure till death do you part. You are with her in sickness and in health, in riches and in poverty, till death do you part.

Two: Avoid separation – Separation in marriage comes in different forms based on the background of the separation. Separation can be based on work, immigration, conflicts, living together but separated (in emotions and communication) as in a roommate situation, etc. As much as possible however, it is good that separation is avoided. The late Pastor Bimbo Odukoya once said: **"don't marry someone you can live with, marry someone you cannot live without"**! A man should so love his wife that he does not want to live a day without her! When a man so loves his wife, the strange woman (Proverbs 5, 6, 7, 9) cannot have any place in his heart, mind, body or pocket (wallet or bank account)! Separation (regardless of purpose) is fertile ground for adultery. Therefore, it should be avoided as much as possible, except in unavoidable circumstances. However, it is possible to overcome adultery in separation because with God, all things are possible (Luke 1:37). Even technology today simplifies the pain of marital separation because calls are now inexpensive via phone apps, video calls are free, etc.

Three: Be patient, kind and understanding – 1 Corinthians 13 summarizes the traits of love which a husband needs to display to his wife regularly. "Charity suffereth long, and is kind; charity envieth not; charity vaunteth not itself, is not puffed up, Doth not behave itself unseemly, seeketh not her own, is not easily provoked, thinketh no evil; Rejoiceth not in iniquity, but rejoiceth in the truth; Beareth all things, believeth all things, hopeth all things, endureth all things" (1 Corinthians 13:4-7). Kindness encourages your wife to be better. **Love, in the form of kindness, makes it easier for her to submit**. Patience shows her in action, that you truly love her in spite of your perception of her shortcomings.

Four: Be a giver – Love gives! "For God so loved the world, that he gave his only begotten Son, that whosoever believeth in him should not perish, but have everlasting life" (John 3:16). You might not have all the money to buy things but there are other things to give – affection, affirmation, etc. "Greater love hath no man than this, that a man lay down his life for his friends" (John 15:13). God wants you to love your wife as much as he loves you. As such, if the need be, he wants you to be able to give your life for her (Ephesians 5:25)! Love is about sacrifice not just about feelings. Love transcends feelings and emotions that the world portrays. Marriages are able to stand the test of time when the love of the husband supersedes emotions and translates to sacrifice.

There are three things men use as safeguards from infidelity: moral, religious, and spiritual reinforcements. Moral reinforcements are those societal norms that have been implanted in you from your youth. This works with our God-given conscience. Some men through their moral upbringings or convictions, resist the lure for infidelity. Naturally, a man (regardless of religiosity or spirituality) who is caught in an extra-marital affair may try to hide because of his sense of guilt. Religious reinforcements are those boundaries set by religion. Through religious commitments, some choose not to engage in extramarital affairs. Spiritual reinforcements deals with the spiritual victory of Christ's death on the cross that brings deliverance over sin and the spiritual transformation of renewing the mind. Saints who are sanctified by the word (John 17:17), have victory of iniquity. Regardless of the safeguard, it is a personal choice to resist sin (James 1: 13-16; James 4:7).

The summary of safeguarding marriage form divorce can be put in two words: **love** and **submission**. When these two words are displayed accurately; passionately; and with the wisdom of God and guidance of the Holy Spirit within a home, there will be no room for divorce regardless of the challenges or obstacles that the marriage will face.

"Now concerning the things whereof ye wrote unto me: It is good for a man not to touch a woman. Nevertheless, to avoid fornication, let every man have his own wife, and let every woman have her own husband. Let the husband render unto the wife *due benevolence*: and likewise also the wife unto the husband. The wife *hath not power of her own body*, but the husband: and likewise also the husband hath not power of his own body, but the wife. Defraud ye not one the other, except it be with consent for a time, that ye may give yourselves to fasting and prayer; and come together again, that Satan tempt you not for your incontinency. But I speak this by permission, and not of commandment. For I would that all men were even as I myself. But every man hath his proper gift of God, one after this manner, and another after that" (1 Corinthians 7:1-7).

"Likewise, ye wives, be in subjection to your own husbands; that, if any obey not the word, they also may without the word be won by the conversation of the wives; While they behold your chaste conversation coupled with fear. Whose adorning let it not be that outward adorning of plaiting the hair, and of wearing of gold, or of putting on of apparel; But let it be the hidden man of the heart, in that which is not corruptible, even the ornament of a meek and quiet spirit, which is in the sight of God of great price. For after this manner in the old time the holy women also, who trusted in God, adorned themselves, being in subjection unto their own husbands: Even as Sara obeyed Abraham, calling him lord: whose daughters ye are, as long as ye do well, and are not afraid with any amazement. Likewise, ye husbands, dwell with them according to knowledge, giving honour unto the wife, as unto the weaker vessel, and as being heirs together of the grace of life; that your prayers be not hindered" (1 Peter 3:1-7).

Ephesians 5: 21-33 says: "**Submitting yourselves one to another in the fear of God. Wives, submit** yourselves unto your own husbands, as unto the Lord. For the husband is the head of the wife, even as Christ is the head of the church: and he is the saviour of the body. Therefore as the church is subject unto Christ, so let the wives be to their own husbands in every thing. **Husbands, love your wives,** even as Christ also loved the church, and gave himself for it; That he might sanctify and cleanse it with the washing of water by the word, That he might present it to himself a glorious church, not having spot, or wrinkle, or any such thing; but that it should be holy and without blemish. **So ought men to love their wives as their own bodies. He that loveth his wife loveth himself.** For no man ever yet hated his own flesh; but nourisheth and cherisheth it, even as the Lord the church: For we are members of his body, of his flesh, and of his bones. For this cause shall a man leave his father and mother, and shall be joined unto his wife, and they two shall be one flesh. This is a great mystery: but I speak concerning Christ and the church. Nevertheless let every one of you in particular **so love his wife even as himself; and the wife see that she reverence her husband**".

But how do we love our wives, submit to our husbands, and submit one to another? It requires a lot of prayer for divine guidance and help (1 Thessalonians 5:17); as well as genuine spirit of humility. "But he giveth more grace. Wherefore he saith, God resisteth the proud, but giveth grace unto the humble" (James 4:6). As for men, the scriptures says that Christ sanctified and cleansed the church with the washing of water by the word. **This means that the woman you married will not be perfect and you, through the love you are commanded to have for her, will help in transforming her into the glorious wife she is destined to be (Ephesians 5:25-27). Instead of complaining about your wife's faults, love her and draw out the greatness in her.**

As earlier stated, submission makes it easier for a husband to love his wife; love also makes it easier for a wife to submit to her husband. What then comes first – love or submission?

Here's a quick exposition of each partner's thought (you might be able to tell who is who by the responses):

One spouse said: The bible says that men should love the wife as Christ loves the church. Christ loved the church before the church even contemplated submission. While we were yet sinners, Christ died (Romans 5:8).

The other said: Every time the bible talks about the roles of the spouses, he commands the wife to submit first, before he commands the husband to love (Ephesians 5, Colossians 3, 1 Peter 3).

Conclusion: From both angles, we concluded that there is no "*if, then clause*", meaning that there is no first or second. The scripture does not say **if** he loves you, **then** submit; neither did it say **if** she submits, **then** love her. The earlier stated examples of Smith Wigglesworth's wife and Mrs. Deborah Powe are clear examples (with results) of submission without love; and the bible example also stated earlier of how Hosea loved Gomer despite her unwillingness to submit to his headship (Hosea 1), is a clear exhibit of love without submission. In these divine commands to spouses, God is impartial. Just as the bible says in Ephesians 5: 21: "**Submitting yourselves one to another in the fear of God**"; and 1 Peter 3:8-9 says "Finally, be ye all of one mind, having compassion one of another, **love as brethren**, be pitiful, be courteous: **Not rendering evil for evil, or railing for railing**: but contrariwise blessing; knowing that ye are thereunto called, that ye should inherit a blessing". In these scriptures, we see how God says to both to submit and both to love. This means that when she is not submitting, you have two roles to play as the husband – submit and love. Likewise, when he is not loving, you have an extra role to play – love your husband. It further says that we should not render evil for evil, meaning that if she does not submit, you should still love; and vice versa. Even Christ on earth played two roles of: love to us (John 3:16), and submission on our behalf (Philippians 2:8) when we did not know how to submit to his will as a sinful world. Now that we know, he expects us to submit to him while he continues to love us (Romans 8:34; Hebrews 7:25).

"For the LORD, the God of Israel, saith that he hateth putting away..." Malachi 2:16

The Bible Message on Divorce

"And it came to pass, that when Jesus had finished these sayings, he departed from Galilee, and came into the coasts of Judaea beyond Jordan; And great multitudes followed him; and he healed them there. The Pharisees also came unto him, tempting him, and saying unto him, Is it lawful for a man to put away his wife for every cause? And he answered and said unto them, Have ye not read, that he which made them at the beginning made them male and female, And said, For this cause shall a man leave father and mother, and shall cleave to his wife: and they twain shall be one flesh? Wherefore they are no more twain, but one flesh. What therefore God hath joined together, let not man put asunder. They say unto him, Why did Moses then command to give a writing of divorcement, and to put her away? He saith unto them, Moses because of the hardness of your hearts suffered you to put away your wives: but from the beginning it was not so. And I say unto you, Whosoever shall put away his wife, except it be for fornication, and shall marry another, committeth adultery: and whoso marrieth her which is put away doth commit adultery. His disciples say unto him, If the case of the man be so with his wife, it is not good to marry. But he said unto them, All men cannot receive this saying, save they to whom it is given. For there are some eunuchs, which were so born from their mother's womb: and there are some eunuchs, which were made eunuchs of men: and there be eunuchs, which have made themselves eunuchs for the kingdom of heaven's sake. He that is able to receive it, let him receive it" (Matthew 19:1-12).

"It hath been said, Whosoever shall put away his wife, let him give her a writing of divorcement: But I say unto you, That whosoever shall put away his wife, saving for the cause of fornication, causeth her to commit adultery: and whosoever shall marry her that is divorced committeth adultery" (Matthew 5:31, 32).

"And the Pharisees came to him, and asked him, Is it lawful for a man to put away his wife? tempting him. And he answered and said unto them, What did Moses command you? And they said, Moses suffered to write a bill of divorcement, and to put her away. And Jesus answered and said unto them, For the hardness of your heart he wrote you this precept. But from the beginning of the creation God made them male and female. For this cause shall a man leave his father and mother, and cleave to his wife; And they twain shall be one flesh: so then they are no more twain, but one flesh. What therefore God hath joined together, let not man put asunder. And in the house his disciples asked him again of the same matter. And he saith unto them, Whosoever shall put away his wife, and marry another, committeth adultery against her. And if a woman shall put away her husband, and be married to another, she committeth adultery" (Mark 10:2-12).

"And unto the married I command, yet not I, but the Lord, Let not the wife depart from her husband: But and if she depart, let her remain unmarried or be reconciled to her husband: and let not the husband put away his wife. But to the rest speak I, not the Lord: If any brother hath a wife that believeth not, and she be pleased to dwell with him, let him not put her away. And the woman which hath an husband that believeth not, and if he be pleased to dwell with her, let her not leave him. For the unbelieving husband is sanctified by the wife, and the unbelieving wife is sanctified by the husband: else were your children unclean; but now are they holy. But if the unbelieving depart, let him depart. A brother or a sister is not under bondage in such cases: but God hath called us to peace. For what knowest thou, O wife, whether thou shalt save thy husband? or how knowest thou, O man, whether thou shalt save thy wife? But as God hath distributed to every man, as the Lord hath called every one, so let him walk. And so ordain I in all churches. Is any man called being circumcised? let him not become uncircumcised. Is any called in uncircumcision? let him not be circumcised. Circumcision is nothing, and uncircumcision is nothing, but the keeping of the commandments of God. Let every man abide in the same calling wherein he was called. Art thou called being a servant? care not for it: but if thou mayest be made free, use it rather. For he that is called in the Lord, being a servant, is the Lord's freeman: likewise also he that is called, being free, is Christ's servant. Ye are bought with a price; be not ye the servants of men. Brethren, let every man, wherein he is called, therein abide with God. Now concerning virgins I have no commandment of the Lord: yet I give my judgment, as one that hath obtained mercy of the Lord to be faithful. I suppose therefore that this is good for the present distress, I say, that it is good for a man so to be. <u>Art thou bound unto a wife? seek not to be loosed. Art thou loosed from a wife? seek not a wife. But and if thou marry, thou hast not sinned; and if a virgin marry, she hath not sinned. Nevertheless such shall have trouble in the flesh: but I spare you.</u> But this I say, brethren, the time is short: it remaineth, that both they that have wives be as though they had none; And they that weep, as though they wept not; and they that rejoice, as though they rejoiced not; and they that buy, as though they possessed not; And they that use this world, as not abusing it: for the fashion of this world passeth away. But I would have you without carefulness. He that is unmarried careth for the things that belong to the Lord, how he may please the Lord: But he that is married careth for the things that are of the world, how he may please his wife. There is difference also between a wife and a virgin. The unmarried woman careth for the things of the Lord, that she may be holy both in body and in spirit: but she that is married careth for the things of the world, how she may please her husband. And this I speak for your own profit; not that I may cast a snare upon you, but for that which is comely, and that ye may attend upon the Lord without distraction. But if any man think that he behaveth himself uncomely toward his virgin, if she pass the flower of her age, and need so require, let him do what he will, he sinneth not: let them marry. Nevertheless he that standeth stedfast in his heart, having no necessity, but hath power over his own will, and hath so decreed in his heart that he will keep his virgin, doeth well. So then he that giveth her in marriage doeth well; but he that giveth her not in marriage doeth better. The wife is bound by the law as long as her husband liveth; but if her husband be dead, she is at liberty to be married to whom she will; only in the Lord. But she is happier if she so abide, after my judgment: and I think also that I have the Spirit of God" (1 Corinthians 7:10-40).

Chapter 8

(ETERNAL DESTINY)

And as it is appointed unto men once to die, but after this the judgement" *(Hebrews 9:27)*

Eternal Destiny

Just like we are all given an earthly destiny to be accomplished in the process of time, every human and even all angels have an eternal destiny: Eternity with God in Heaven or the Lake of Fire with the Devil. The process of attaining one's eternal destiny is in two parts. The first part was completed on the Cross of Calvary over two thousand years ago by Jesus when He said "it is finished" (John 19:30). The second part lies in the hand of each individual. Either you accept Jesus now and live for Him all the days of your life to make heaven, or you refuse and rebel into eternal damnation (Isaiah 1:18-20). **The choice is yours to make and the consequence to take**. The angels have already settled their eternal accounts as one third led by the devil chose an eternal destiny in the Lake of Fire and the other two thirds were wiser to stick with what's better (Revelation 12:7-12; Revelation 20:10). As long as you are still alive and are reading this book, you still have this rare opportunity to make your eternal choice and settle the matter of your eternal destiny. God has made available two eternal destinies for all (including angels). For man, "it is appointed unto men once to die, but after this the judgment" (Hebrews 9:27). For angels, the case has been settled with no opportunity for repentance for fallen angels now known as demons. For man, despite our fall, the redemptive plan of salvation permits us to access an eternal destiny with God as long as we accept Jesus and live a holy life for him. Without holiness, no man shall see the Lord (Hebrews 12:14). God's standards cannot be lowered. Since He did all for our salvation and redemption by leaving the glory in heaven, taking upon the likeness of man and dying a shameful and painful death on a cross in the hands of his creatures, we have to meet him at **the cross – the halfway line between man and God** (John 3:16). God made arrangements for our Eternal Destiny with him on the cross. Are we going to meet Him there? The devil has also made serious arrangements for our Eternal Destiny in the Lake of Fire with him through all his devices (2 Corinthians 2:11; 1 Peter 5:8).

"For what shall it profit a man, if he shall gain the whole world, and lose his own soul?" (Mark 8:36)

The Eternal Question

Life's journey here on earth has an end. No matter how old you become, how much wealth you gain or how much success you attain here on earth, life on earth ends in the grave and a new phase of life begins elsewhere forever. Therein begins eternity.

Eternity has no end. There are only 2 eternal places of abode – hell and heaven. The former is a disastrous place to be and the latter is a place of peace.

It is appointed unto man once to die and after that the judgment (Hebrews 9:27). Some people do not even live to 15 years before they are faced with eternity. Eternity can come SUDDENLY. That's why you must be prepared for eternity today. Do not live a careless life. You can make your choice today – hell or heaven?

Heaven is a prepared place for prepared people. No one gets to heaven by chance but by choice. Heaven is an eternal abode of peace, joy and the fullness of the presence of God. Hell on the other hand is the extreme opposite – a place of anguish, torments, regrets and frustration <u>for the endless ages of eternity</u>. Hell is not meant for you; it is an eternal abode of destruction. Make your decision today. WHERE WILL YOU SPEND YOUR ETERNITY? Death without Jesus is a disaster. You've got to be ready today.

> <u>*For what shall it profit a man, if he shall gain the whole world, and lose his own soul? Or what shall a man give in exchange for his soul?*</u> (Mark 8:36, 37).

Be sure to make the right decision today. Make sure to get yourself the right eternal address today (Heaven). You can do that by inviting Jesus to your heart right now and confessing Him as your Lord. Truly repent from all evil - He will give you the grace to live above sin (John 1:12).

"For whosoever shall call upon the name of the Lord shall be saved" (Romans 10:13)

Prayer of Salvation

If you truly want to receive Jesus into your heart and be born again, simply pray this prayer genuinely from the depth of your heart and the Lord will hear you, answer you and welcome you home:

"Lord Jesus, I believe you are the son of God, I believe you came to earth two thousand years ago, I believe you died on a cross for me, I believe you rose again on the third day and you are now seated on the right hand of God the Father, and I believe you are coming back again, as the King of kings and the Lord of lords. Dear Lord, come into my heart, wash away my sins with your blood, make me clean and I shall be clean. Thank you for coming into my heart, making me a part of the Bride of Christ and writing my name in the book of life (Amen)".

"Therefore if any man be in Christ, he is a new creature: old things are passed away; behold, all things are become new" (2 Corinthians 5:17)

Now that you are Saved

Now that you are saved by accepting Jesus into your heart as Lord and Saviour, you need to grow in the Lord and maintain a good relationship with His Spirit. To be a good Christian, you need to: get yourself a bible and read it daily so God can speak to you through His word; join a bible believing church so you can fellowship with other believers and grow spiritually; and pray everyday because God wants to hear you speak to Him and prayer is the way we speak to Him. Jesus Christ Himself will give you the grace to live above sin (John 1:12). I look forward to seeing you in Heaven.

You are blessed!